Loving
WITHOUT A
LICENSE

An Estate Planning Survival Guide for Unmarried Couples and Same Sex Partners

PEGGY R. HOYT, J.D., M.B.A.

AND CANDACE M. POLLOCK, J.D.

Forward by Buck Harris

Loving Without a License

An Estate Planning Survival Guide for Unmarried Couples and Same Sex Partners

ISBN 0-9719177-3-6

Copyright © 2004 by Peggy R. Hoyt and Candace M. Pollock

Published by Legacy Planning Partners, LLC

251 Plaza Drive, Suite B

Oviedo, Florida 32765

Phone (407) 977-8080

Facsimile (407) 977-8078

DEDICATION

This book is dedicated to Joe and Hutch, our life alliance partners.
Without your love and support this book would not have been possible.

In addition, we wish to dedicate *Loving Without a License*
to all unmarried couples and same-sex partners who have the courage,
the stamina and the heart to seek legal recognition for the
relationships we hold so dear.

For more information or to order a copy of this book,
visit www.lovingwithoutalicense.com
or call 407.977.8080 or 216.861.6160

The publishing of this book should not be construed as legal, accounting or other professional advice. If legal advice or other professional services are needed or required, please seek the services of a licensed, competent professional.

The hiring of a lawyer is an important decision that should not be based solely upon advertisements. Before you decide, ask us to send you free written information about our qualifications and experience.

Book Design by Julie Hoyt Dorman

www.dormangraphics.com

$\mathcal{T}$ABLE OF $\mathcal{C}$ONTENTS

Forward v

Introduction vii

Chapter 1   The State of the Union 1

Chapter 2   The Law and Your Relationship 7

Chapter 3   The Automatic Wedding Gift 17

Chapter 4   In Sickness or In Health 31

Chapter 5   Until Death Do Us Part 55

Chapter 6   Taxation and Gifts to Uncle Sam 83

Chapter 7   Life Alliance Agreements™ 95

Chapter 8   Solutions for Life Alliance Partners —
A Matter of Trust 113

Chapter 9   Fiduciaries, Attorneys and Other
Scary People 133

Chapter 10   The Paper Trail—Asset Integration
and Funding 153

Chapter 11   Keeping it All Together — Updating,
Education and Maintenance 161

Chapter 12   The End of the Road or Part of the Journey? . . . 171

Appendix A   Glossary of Estate Planning Terms 175

Appendix B   Estate Planning Checklist 181

About the Authors 187

Contact Us 190

$\mathscr{F}$ORWARD

A few weeks ago the authors asked me if I would consider reading a draft of this book and then offer some comment. I agreed to do so without hesitation. I found myself picking up the manuscript with the intentions of plowing through it. Within minutes, I'd find a more pressing task.

Reading this book brought back very unpleasant memories. In 1984, I was appointed by Ohio's Governor Celeste to serve as the Gay Health Consultant to the Ohio Department of Health. My primary responsibility was to head up the AIDS prevention programs throughout the state. My partner Don and I had been together for 8 years when he was diagnosed with full-blown AIDS. We were devastated. He died in 1986. Amazingly, I was uninfected. Don did not have a will. We were in denial and I was terribly naive. I got along well with his brother and sister and so expected they would treat me with the due respect of a spouse. Naturally, I would get all of our savings, the house, the insurance, and my share of a vacation property that we owned jointly with them, even though (for tax purposes) everything was in Don's name. WRONG! I did get the house (which had little equity), one third of the savings, no insurance, and my name was removed from the deed of the vacation property. When Don died, I lost a lot more than my life partner!

But that was then and this is now. Times are much different, society is much more tolerant. And couples are much more sophisticated. WRONG!

This book isn't just a nice read, it's a *must* read. Reading this book has forced me to look at my current circumstances and made me realize that I need to get to work on the Estate Planning Checklist at the back of the book.

Because there are so few institutions that validate life alliance partners, be they same-sex or not, we tend to do little to validate them ourselves. With this book in hand, we may now turn to the one institution that will not only validate, but protect our unions, the profession of law.♥

Buck Harris served as the Gay Health Consultant for the Ohio Department of Health from 1984 until 1996. During that time he launched the first commercial live gay talk show in the country on Cleveland radio station WHK. He now finds life much more serene as the owner of "There's No Place Like OM," a yoga studio.

$\mathscr{I}$NTRODUCTION

This book was written during a period of turmoil regarding the rights of unmarried opposite-sex and same-sex couples. Despite the introduction of some domestic partner laws, civil unions and civil marriages for same-sex couples, any unmarried same or opposite-gender couple in a long-term, committed relationship must take extra steps to obtain protections and benefits that come almost automatically to married couples.

Unmarried partners are particularly vulnerable in the areas of disability and estate planning. The laws don't provide them with the same safety nets that married couples can invoke. Failure to take steps to protect yourself and your loved ones can expose you or your loved ones to unnecessary emotional and financial hardship and prevent you from taking advantage of opportunities to maximize your assets and protections.

Everyone—married and unmarried alike—has an "estate plan" whether they know it or not and regardless of whether their assets are generous or modest. Few people realize they are doing estate planning every time they name a beneficiary on a retirement account or create a joint title on a deed to a house or bank account.

Estate planning basically boils down to creating a combination of *directives* to authorize others to manage and direct your affairs when you are incapacitated, and at your death. Wills and trusts, healthcare proxies and living wills, deeds and beneficiary forms are just some of the common directives that may be included in your plan. The number and type of directives can be complex or simple, depending on your needs, goals and budget.

The key to *good* estate planning is making sure your plan is complete and understanding how each directive supports or undermines your overall intentions. If your plan has gaps or conflicts, state laws will dictate what happens to you and your affairs. For unmarried partners, gaps and conflicts can produce wholly unintended outcomes. If a couple fails to create estate planning directives, state laws will dictate who can speak for the disabled or deceased partner. Under these state laws, next of kin have greater standing than unmarried partners—even when next of kin have been estranged from the disabled or deceased partner.

Proper estate planning can help you maintain control and independence and achieve your goals. To do this you need to 1) identify your goals for taking care of yourself and your loved ones when you are no longer available to do so—either through incapacity or death; 2) understand your planning options; and 3) coordinate your directives to eliminate planning conflicts and gaps.

There are a number of goals legal directives can address. The most common are:

1) Avoiding probate or guardianship and maintaining privacy;
2) Providing for minor children;
3) Providing for special needs family members in such a way that they remain eligible for public benefit programs;
4) Protecting assets from nursing home costs and other catastrophic illness costs;
5) Minimizing state and federal estate taxes.

It should go without saying that the need to create a good, sound foundation for planning for loved ones is certainly not unique to unmarried partners. However, the need to create special directives for the unique needs of unmarried partners requires special attention by estate planners and financial advisors. Unfortunately, most estate planners and financial advisors have limited experience in dealing with these unique needs, and it is easy for them to apply concepts regularly used for married couples to unmarried partners' situations.

Look in the index of most reference books on estate planning and you won't find a section covering "unmarried partners." If you find "unmarried" in the index, you will normally be directed to the section that discusses planning for "single" people.

Unmarried partners are neither fish nor fowl. Sure, in the eyes of the law, unmarried couples are technically single, but "single" doesn't adequately represent the reality of their relationship or their planning needs. Planning as if an unmarried couple were composed of two single persons will not address areas of vulnerability. Planning as if an unmarried couple were married will not be possible due to the numerous techniques that only married people can use. Planning for unmarried couples in committed relationships requires more than the standard approaches offer. If unmarried partners do not raise certain issues, the advisors can sometimes make inappropriate assumptions that will produce a plan that is not truly a good fit for the couple—or at least not the fit the couple should have.

Estate planning decisions straddle legal, financial and other advisor categories. This book is intended as an overview of the many considerations and options across those categories that might be available to unmarried partners. It has been our experience in advising clients over the years that if they understand, in general terms, how a legal process works and where they might fall within that process, they tend to be better consumers and more confident about their choices. We intend to provoke thoughts and questions that couples can consider as they enter the planning process—about what they want and what they need to achieve for themselves and their loved ones.

This is a book for laypeople. Although the material necessarily involves a lot of complex concepts, we have attempted to eliminate legalese whenever possible. We include a glossary in Appendix A with terms that are used during the planning process. The definitions are intended for the layperson and not for legal scholars. In most circumstances, we do not cite case law and regulations since this is not intended to be a legal treatise.

There are a number of terms or phrases used to describe unmarried partners. The terms can have special meaning to some groups and not others. There might not be consensus within the groups as to what the special meanings might be. We have coined the term "life alliance partner" as a neutral label to describe unmarried couples of the same or opposite-gender who are in committed relationships.

There are times we will need to make a distinction between opposite-gender and same-gender couples or partners. We do this for a couple of reasons. In talking with advisors and clients of all varieties, we often experience two things:

- When the term "domestic partner" is used, many opposite-gender unmarried partners can tend to think it only refers to same-gender couples. Consequently, they can fail to appreciate that they need to pay attention to the discussion for themselves. Therefore, we might occasionally remind the reader that a particular concept applies to opposite-gender couples, too.
- While same and opposite-gender couples have many needs and concerns in common, same-gender couples obviously have needs and concerns unique to them. Therefore, it is important to be able to distinguish between these two groups from time to time.

We gratefully acknowledge our many colleagues who have contributed their insights, wisdom and inspiration on this topic over the years. We appreciate all of them as we certainly share a common bond—a genuine concern for people and their unique needs. It would be impossible to properly credit them for the work, ideas and expressions of philosophy that we have woven into our practices from education conferences, articles, legal chat rooms and phone calls. We have endeavored to determine whether previously published material included in this book requires permission to reprint. Please accept our apologies if there has been any failure to provide proper credit or if there has been an error or omission of any kind. We will be happy to make corrections in subsequent editions. ♥

Chapter 1

The State of the Union

sk people about their idea of the typical family in the United States and they will probably describe the stereotype of the pre-1960s "traditional family" composed of two parents of opposite-gender, married to each other, with one or more children. This stereotype was represented in television shows such as *Leave it to Beaver, Ozzie and Harriet* and *Father Knows Best*. Although many families in the Ozzie and Harriet era did not fit that traditional mold, the prevailing view was that it was the typical and preferred family structure to which everyone aspired and against which all other relationships were judged.

The bias toward the traditional family structure was reflected in everything: advertising, music, television, financial products and services as well as laws regarding inheritances, employment benefits, credit and insurance proceeds. People whose family unit did not fit the traditional mold generally had little expectation that industry or laws would address their unique needs. Instead, many attempted to duplicate, as best they could, the benefits available to married couples.

Over the last forty years, family diversity has come close to being the norm. The traditional family, as we think we knew it, seems to be becoming the minority. In place of the traditional family, we have family units of all varieties: single parents, who have either never married or are single due to death or divorce;

married couples with or without children; married couples in their second or more marriage with or without blended families; and unmarried couples of either the same or opposite-gender, with or without children, in long-term committed relationships. Some relationship categories are so prevalent that they are identified by their own acronym, such as "DINK" for dual income, no kids.

Social scientists tell us these changes are due to many factors including the increase in divorce rates, the increase in population mobility, the decrease in the social stigma against being single, the increase in single parenthood, the increase in earning power for women, the acceptance of same-gender relationships, and longer life expectancies.

Among these groups, the number of opposite-gender couples who live together in long-term committed relationships continues to increase. United States Census data from 2002 shows a 4.5% increase in unmarried couples and a 3% decrease in married couples.

At one time, statisticians said that unmarried opposite-sex couples tended to get married within two to three years of living together. Living together was seen as a trial period before marriage and permitted the couple to save money more quickly, the theory being that two can live cheaper than one.

Over time, however, statistics have shown that the period of time such couples remain together in the unmarried state has lengthened. Some common reasons this group gives for remaining unmarried:

- Emotional trauma from prior failed relationship(s) or marriage(s)

- Marriage is not permitted for same-sex relationships
- Desire to avoid IRS "marriage penalty" on income taxation
- Loss of widow/widower benefits upon remarriage

At the same time, same-gender couples in committed, live-in relationships have also increased in numbers. The increase might merely reflect society's awareness of this group, in addition to an actual increase in the numbers of such couples due to greater societal acceptance and other factors.

Consumer products, advertising, articles of interest and other services may have evolved over recent years to focus on the needs of life alliance partners. However, despite such changes, biases in favor of married couples persist. A life alliance partnership's ability to reliably duplicate the range of benefits routinely available to married couples is hard to achieve, even in current times.

It has been reported that the status of marriage conveys a potential one thousand (1,000) or more rights for each partner in a marriage.[1] This number may actually be higher and growing. These rights can include anything from automatic inheritances for surviving spouses to discounts on health insurance premiums.

Currently, there are no laws that automatically permit partners in a committed, long-term, yet unmarried, relationship, to achieve comparable protections and standing in the eyes of the law. And, in fact, some laws have been passed to specifically prevent unmarried couples from achieving equal status. Certainly, this is true for same-sex couples.

Chapter 3 will more fully explain the access to rights and privileges married people automatically receive upon getting married. Opposite-sex, unmarried couples have always had the option of availing themselves of these rights simply by getting married. Unmarried, same-sex partners, on the other hand, cannot currently do so.

It is an understatement to say that the laws regarding unmarried partners of same or opposite-gender are currently undergoing radical changes. These changes are occurring at the local, state, national and international levels, and even in the private sector. For example:

- Over 5,000 employers provide family-type benefits to employees in unmarried partnerships, although some limit such benefits to same-sex partners on the theory that opposite-sex partners can marry to obtain the benefits. Public-sector employers are less likely to extend benefits to either category of unmarried partners.[2]

- Some communities now have "domestic partner registries" that permit unmarried couples to be publicly listed as committed partners and receive a certificate of registration. The certificate does not guarantee rights to registrants, but gives the couple some "proof" of their committed status.

- Officials with the City of San Francisco performed civil marital or "marriage" ceremonies between same-sex couples even though the ceremonies currently have no legal effect.

- Vermont passed legislation permitting civil unions between same-sex partners.

- Hawaii and California provide state benefits to same-sex couples that are comparable to those provided to married couples.
- Ohio passed legislation preventing Ohio from recognizing same-sex unions regardless of where they are performed, and from extending the legal benefits of marriage to unmarried couples.
- The Massachusetts Superior Court ruled that the Massachusetts law limiting marriage to opposite-sex partners was unconstitutional because it violated the U.S. Constitution's right to equal protection and due process for all citizens. The Court found that gay and lesbian couples are entitled to the "protections, benefits, and obligations of civil marriage."[3] The court stayed this ruling for six months to permit the Massachusetts legislature time to "take such action as it may deem appropriate in light of this opinion." It is has been reported that the first same-sex marriages may be authorized in Massachusetts before the end of 2004.
- The federal 1996 Defense of Marriage Act (DOMA) says that the term "married person(s)" appearing in any federal law or regulation only means people of the opposite-gender. It also says that states are not required to recognize same-sex marriages validly performed in other states.
- The U.S. President, George W. Bush, is urging the legislature to pass a constitutional amendment banning same-sex marriages.
- Canada legalized same-sex marriages in 2003.

The domestic partner registries, Vermont law and the Massachusetts Supreme Court ruling are steps toward giving life alliance partners greater standing and legitimacy in the eyes of the law. However, a civil union is not the same as a marriage and, consequently, will not automatically convey the full range of protections and privileges triggered by obtaining married status alone. Additionally, these actions at the state level will not entitle life alliance partners to federal benefits under the Social Security rules for survivors or other federal laws.

Current and future legislation on the rights, privileges and limitations regarding life alliance partners is destined to work its way through the legislative and legal process. Ultimately, the U.S. Supreme Court will help resolve the "law of the land." This will be a lengthy process. Until such time as the process is complete, life alliance partners must continue to take extra steps to obtain protections for themselves and their loved ones. They cannot assume that the laws passed, even in their own jurisdictions, will ultimately prevail. They should diligently prepare legal directives to memorialize their intentions and to put themselves in the best position to overcome hurdles that future legislation might place in their way.

The legal forces that shape or inhibit the rights and obligations of any U.S. citizen consist of more than statutes or court decisions. It is important to understand some of these factors in the context of planning for unmarried partners to better appreciate how and why some options are available or some consequences could occur regardless of what the couple had in mind. Chapter 2 describes some of the general forces that come to bear on the relationships of life alliance partners. ♥

Chapter 2

The Law and Your Relationship

Married or unmarried, it is easy to lose sight of the many layers of laws and legal principles that govern our daily existence in the United States. Until we "bump" into the invisible walls they create, we can fail to appreciate how many legal arenas our everyday activities straddle. There are many legal rules and theories that can be brought to bear when addressing the relationship and planning needs of life alliance partners. Many unintended consequences can result when life alliance partners share households, co-mingle assets, create joint title to assets and share expenses. By the very nature of the married status, the same actions performed by married couples produce very different consequences.

In a famous 1976 court case, Marvin v. Marvin, movie actor Lee Marvin was found financially liable to his former live-in girlfriend when the relationship ended. The term "palimony," a play on the word "alimony," was coined and has come to represent the bundle of rights and benefits an unmarried partner might seek from the other partner when the relationship ends.

Relying on several legal theories, such as contractual rights and principles of equity, the court found that the girlfriend should receive compensation rather than leave the long-term relationship "empty-handed." Prior to Marvin, unmarried, cohabiting partners whose relationship ended had no legal rights to each other's property. The Marvin case was a signal to unmarried couples that the courts could look at the actions of the parties to determine whether there were elements of implied contract, partnership or joint venture, constructive trust or *quantum meruit*. Although the <u>Marvin</u> decision and its rationale are not followed in every jurisdiction, some states have expanded the <u>Marvin</u> court's holding to permit same-sex partners similar remedies.

This case and others like it illustrate how an unmarried couple's everyday activities can trigger unforeseen outcomes and consequences. Long-standing legal principles can be cobbled together in unique ways to produce new theories of "relatedness," obligation and liability between unmarried partners— regardless of the presence of statutory provisions or the absence of such provisions. Add this to the application of existing probate, taxation and disability rules, and unmarried partners can find they are inadvertently causing tax and other consequences they never considered. Therefore, it is important to understand the legal landscape to properly navigate the theories and options life alliance partners need for their own benefit and protection.

The following is a brief discussion of some of the more prominent concepts that can come to bear on planning for life alliance partners. This is not an exhaustive list by any means, however.

Common Law, Codified Law And Case Law

In the United States we operate under a legal system that is a mix of common law, codified law and court decisions.

The common law is a body of laws, written and unwritten, and legal theories that were developed in England through common usage, customs and court judgments that affirmed and enforced the usages and customs. A portion of the English common law was adopted in the United States during the American Revolution.

Codified law is the body of written laws created through the legislative process at the local, state and federal levels. These are sometimes referred to as the "black letter law" or the "code."

Case law refers to the body of decisions courts issue when deciding legal matters before them. The courts will apply common or codified law to the specific fact situations presented. The court decisions interpret, clarify and sometimes obscure, enforce or reject the rules presented by such laws. Thereafter, other parties to court actions can refer to the body of written decisions to identify the latest interpretation of the common or codified laws in their jurisdiction. Case law in one jurisdiction might not be identical to case law in other jurisdictions.

Full Faith And Credit, Conflict Of Laws And Superior Authority

The phrase "full faith and credit" refers to Article 4, Section 1 of the U.S. Constitution which requires states to recognize the public acts, records and judicial proceedings of every other state.

The Legislature is empowered to prescribe the manner in which such acts, records and proceedings are provided and the effect of the proof received. This means that a person who is married is New Jersey and then moves to Florida still has a valid marriage. Likewise, legal documents created in one state should be recognized in another state. A divorce in one state is recognized as a divorce in another state. For this reason, it is not entirely uncommon for people to choose a state whose laws offer favorable consequences and then to take advantage of those laws. One example might be choosing a state where no blood test or waiting period is required before getting a marriage license instead of a state where a blood test or waiting period is required.

Case law has created exceptions to the full faith and credit doctrine where honoring actions performed under the foreign state's laws would violate the state's strong public policy.

"Conflict of laws" arises when the laws of different jurisdictions apply to the case at hand and the laws do not agree as to the rights and remedies available to the parties. In this situation, the court(s) with authority to decide the matter must determine whether and which set of laws apply or trump the other and what remedies will be permitted.

"Superior authority" refers to the concept that some laws and some courts will have higher authority than others. In other words, the legislative and judicial systems have a hierarchy of authority where the enactments or decisions of one will prevail over the enactments or decisions at a lower level. It is important to understand how law conflicts work their way through the various courts and which ones prevail as "the law of the land."

Bodies Of Law

The 1,000-plus rights afforded to married couples mostly involve surviving spouse benefits under a number of federal laws. Therefore, the 1,000 figure is a bit misleading. When discussing the various rights married couples or life alliance partners might have, it helps to put them into categories by body of law. The major bodies of law are probate laws (including inheritance, guardianship and some domestic relations), general disability planning (including health care and financial issues) and tax laws.

There are federal laws, state laws and local laws that may overlap, coexist or conflict regarding the rights and obligations of life alliance partners. Planning for life alliance partners requires advisors to coordinate directives to take advantage of laws in favor of the life alliance partners and avoid the disadvantages of unfavorable laws.

Probate Laws. Each state has its own probate code. The probate code in most states controls disability determinations and the guardianship or incapacity process, sometimes referred to as "living probate," when there is no private mechanism in place to address mental incapacity.

The probate laws also set forth the rules for inheritance, either via a will or without one. The probate court will hear contested matters regarding inheritances and supervise or oversee the payment of creditors and the distribution of assets.

Domestic Relations Laws. Each state has its own laws regarding the relations, rights and obligations of family members. This includes marriage and divorce, parentage, custody, support issues, adoptions and name changes.

Disability Laws. Unlike probate laws or domestic relation laws, laws pertaining to an individual's physical or mental disability can be interspersed among a variety of bodies of laws. Probate laws, as mentioned above, will be one such body of laws. There can be other laws regarding adult or elder abuse; Medicaid rules; healthcare provider rules; and workers' compensation or Social Security Disability benefits, depending on the situation at hand.

Tax Laws. Federal income, gift and estate tax laws will apply to all citizens. Some states also have income and estate or inheritance tax laws. Married couples have several advantages under federal tax laws. Unmarried couples can create directives to mimic these advantages, but the advantages won't occur without proper planning.

The Court Systems

The court systems in the United States can be categorized by a number of methods. The categories pertinent to our discussion are as follows:

- Hierarchy of jurisdiction or authority; namely, federal, state and county. There are sub-tiers of hierarchies within jurisdictions as well, such as lower level actions, appeal level courts and the highest level appeal courts;
- Civil courts, including the sub-categories of civil courts such as probate, domestic relations and common pleas; and
- Although not technically a court system, alternative dispute-resolution methods, such as mediation or

arbitration, exist in and around the court systems to expedite the resolution of disputes that might otherwise end up in the court system.

Legal Doctrines

A legal doctrine is a "rule, principal, theory, or tenet of the law."[4] There are many legal doctrines that can be applied to the interests of life alliance partners—either in their best interests or against them. Some of the most obvious doctrines are below:

Contract. A contract is an agreement between two or more parties to do or not to do a particular thing. Contracts must have an offer, an acceptance and consideration (something of value) to back them up. The consideration to support the contract could be the mutual promises of the parties to the contract. Parties to a contract must be legally competent, there must be mutuality of agreement and the contract cannot be so vague that its terms are not ascertainable.

General contract principles can be discussed according to sub-categories. This list is not complete, but illustrates the categories that would be most likely to appear in the context of planning for life alliance partners.

Conditional Contract. The performance of the contract depends on the occurrence of a contingency—in other words, something either must happen or not happen for the contract to be valid.

Constructive Contract. This is a contract that is deduced from the actions of the parties even if all of the formalities of a contract have not been met. This is similar to the equitable doctrine of implied contract.

Express Contract. This is a contract that is explicit and is an actual agreement of the parties. Generally, an express contract will also be written.

Implied Contract. This is a contract that is inferred from the conduct of the parties and the circumstances surrounding the transaction. This is similar to a constructive contract.

Equity: Equity is the quality of being fair and just. In law, equity refers to the application of principles of justice and fairness to resolve the dispute at hand. It is an ethical obligation rather than a legal obligation.[5] In other words, where the written statutes or case law is silent or in conflict, the decision-maker (arbitrator or judge) will look to equitable principles to resolve the matter at hand.

The principles of equity often fill in the gaps. In the case where a contract is silent regarding damages in the event of a breach of the contract, equity will permit compensation to the party who suffered damages as a result of the breach.

Operation of Law. This refers to a legal mechanism where the rights or liabilities of the parties to a matter are invoked without the act or cooperation of the parties. A familiar example of this is where property is held in "joint tenancy with rights of survivorship" (JTROS or sometimes, JTWROS) and title automatically vests in the surviving owner(s) upon the death of a joint title owner.

Putative. This is a term that means "commonly assumed or reputed."[6] In the context of life alliance planning, the term is used to refer to "putative spouse;" in other words, a spouse in many ways except by formal standards or statute.

Quantum Meruit. This is a Latin term that roughly means "for what it is worth."[7] It is an equitable doctrine that refers to the concept that parties to an implied contract should pay or be paid what is deserved regardless of any agreement or failure of an agreement as to value. An example might be if someone paints your house and you fail to pay. The painter is entitled to some compensation for the value of the services provided.

Unjust Enrichment. This term generally refers to the concept that one should not gain by trickery or some other unfair advantage in a transaction.[8] If gain was achieved by trickery and a dispute arises, the application of fairness would permit decision-makers to find an equitable outcome even if the document or applicable laws do not address such an outcome.

The point of this chapter is to illustrate that these are just some of the many legal doctrines and principles that can be used to gain or defeat legal rights or protections for life alliance partners—regardless of what the partners intended or thought they were creating. Therefore, it is important that unmarried partners get the advice of experts in estate planning or financial planning to be sure they are well protected.

Some principles from business law might also offer some planning solutions for life alliance partners and can be applied as well. For example, life alliance partners can create a business partnership, limited liability company, limited partnership and/or buy-sell agreements. They will be required to meet the filing and reporting standards of the business entity they have selected. These alternatives will be discussed in greater depth in Chapter 8.

Some areas of planning need particular attention in order for life alliance partners to take advantage of opportunities and minimize dangers that could threaten their independence. All solutions should be evaluated to determine whether they address these areas of planning:

- to achieve the couple's estate planning and financial goals and meet their needs during health;
- to manage these estate planning and financial goals through one or both partners' incapacity;
- to address the needs of the partners and their loved ones when one or both partners die; and
- to avoid unintended estate planning and financial consequences that can occur when unmarried partners co-mingle funds and share the normal expenses of living together.

Keep in mind when reading the following chapters that many theories of "relatedness" and entitlement can be invoked or defeated by relying on some of the principles in this chapter. But first, it helps to understand where married couples have advantages that life alliance partners might want to duplicate. These advantages are outlined in Chapter 3. ♥

Chapter 3

The Automatic Wedding Gift

*R*odney Dangerfield-type humor aside, marriage has many advantages. For one, a married couple normally gets gifts to help them establish a household together. However, one of the biggest gifts a married couple receives that doesn't come gift-wrapped is the bundle of rights and protections each partner to the marriage receives as soon as the marriage ceremony is complete.

As stated in Chapter 1, some sources estimate that the married status triggers a potential 1,000 plus rights. Some of the most familiar are:

- protections under probate inheritance laws;
- preferences under rules for healthcare and disability proxies;
- ability to transfer substantial sums to one another without a gift or estate tax liability;
- survivor's benefits under pension, retirement and the Social Security system; and
- alimony and other rights to the other spouse's property upon termination of a marriage

Life alliance partners do not receive these rights or benefits automatically. However, they can create many similar protections and benefits with proper planning. First, let us more fully explain some of the types of benefits we can try to duplicate or improve upon.

States retain authority to recognize marriage as the legal union between two people. This legal union then defines the rights and responsibilities of the couple toward each other and in the eyes of the law.

The "big three" areas of benefits involve preferences regarding property rights, inheritance and taxation.

Property Rights

Tenancy by the Entireties

Tenancy by the entirety (TBE) is a form of joint ownership available only to husbands and wives. It is not recognized in all states. Some states used to recognize tenancy by the entirety but no longer do. However, these states will recognize tenancy by the entirety deeds that were properly created before tenancy by the entirety was abolished in their state.

Here, when a married couple acquires property in their joint names with the added notation that they are husband and wife, the law provides some benefits that go beyond simple survivorship. Some states protect tenancy by the entirety property from a spouse's creditors. The creditor has to have a valid judgment against both spouses before the property can be subject to attachment. This protection can be especially important for couples when one or both work in a high-liability type of profession, such as doctor, lawyer, engineer or architect. Tenancy by the entirety protection, however, is not always automatic and financial institutions are not always familiar with the benefits of this form of ownership.

Community Property

There are eight states in the nation that have community property laws. In a community property state, all property earned or obtained during the marriage is assumed to belong to both parties, regardless of how the property is titled. In addition, community property laws

8 States that Recognize Community Property Laws
1) California
2) Arizona
3) Washington
4) Wisconsin
5) Idaho
6) Louisiana
7) Nevada
8) New Mexico

provide some tax benefits at the death of the first spouse under rules that permit a "full step-up" in basis for the value of the property to the fair market value on the date the deceased spouse died. This allows the surviving spouse to avoid paying capital gains taxes on the difference between the original acquisition price and the fair market value of the asset on the date it is sold.

Dower/Curtesy

Most states have abolished the rules governing dower and curtesy. These are old common law rights that evolved to protect the property interests of wives (dower) and husbands (curtesy) in the event that a spouse died without a will. Today, these rules have been replaced in many jurisdictions by a state's "elective share rights," discussed later in this chapter.

The rules governing dower and curtesy provided that a spouse could not convey (give, sell or otherwise transfer) property without the consent of the other spouse. If a transfer of property was attempted without the other spouse's consent, the non-consenting spouse retained a right to a portion of the property.

Corporate Benefits

Public and private corporations offer a host of benefits to their employees. Many of these benefits, like health insurance, life insurance and medical-leave provisions extend to spouses and children of the employees. Some corporations are starting to recognize the unmarried partners of employees although, as previously mentioned, some limit such provisions to same-sex partners under the theory that opposite-sex partners can get married to obtain the desired benefits.

Pensions and Social Security

The rules governing pensions and Social Security benefits are uniquely geared toward married individuals. Generally, pensions provide benefits only to surviving spouses at the death of a worker. If benefits are payable to non-spouses, the payout options are not as favorable as they would be for a surviving spouse. Social Security retirement benefits provide survivor benefits only to spouses and children.

Divorce

When a married couple wants to end their relationship, they must get a divorce. Divorce is normally considered a bad thing. However, the positive side of divorce is that it provides a court-supervised process for dividing property between spouses. The process is supposed to increase the likelihood that a spouse who contributed homemaking and family care services rather than tangible assets to the relationship is not overly disadvantaged when the relationship ends.

A divorce invokes the laws of the state in which the couple

seeks the divorce. Each state's rules governing the distribution of property, the payment of support or alimony, the payment of child support, and so forth are different.

Premarital agreements have the effect of modifying these state rules, and can be beneficial when a relationship ends, but there is always the risk that a premarital agreement will challenged by one of the parties and might not be enforced.

Inheritance Rights

Laws That Protect a Spouse's Elective Share

There are a number of laws, both federal and state, that protect spouses. One we've already mentioned above—dower and curtesy: the right to inherit property from a spouse that dies without a will or a trust. Some states have passed laws that provide similar protections. These are called elective share rights. These statutes prevent one spouse from intentionally or unintentionally omitting the other spouse from a will.

In Florida, if your spouse makes a will or trust and tries to disinherit you, the spousal elective share protects your right to at least 30% of the deceased person's estate. In earlier versions of this law, the 30% only applied to the deceased's probate estate. Therefore, an individual could avoid the effect of the law simply by creating a trust or using other legal titling mechanisms to avoid creating a probate estate. Today, the definition of "elective estate"—the estate the surviving spouse has an entitlement to—has been expanded to include, with a few exceptions, the deceased's worldwide assets.

Probate Preferences

Each state's intestacy statutes protect heirs when a person dies without a will. Intestacy statutes are designed to keep families from being completely disinherited. These laws generally provide for surviving spouses and children or grandchildren (lineal descendants). Intestacy statutes do not provide for unrelated persons, such as a life alliance partner.

Taxes

Historically, married couples have been subject to the "marriage penalty" for income tax purposes. This means that a married couple actually pays more taxes than two unmarried individuals with the same combined earnings. However, the disadvantage of the marriage penalty is generally outweighed by the advantages married couples enjoy under other tax rules regarding unlimited gifts and the "unlimited marital deduction."

From an estate tax perspective, a married person can leave an unlimited value of assets to his or her U.S.-citizen spouse. This is called the "unlimited marital deduction." This means that Bill Gates can leave his entire fortune to his wife, and at the time of his death there will be no estate tax due on the value transferred to his wife. The estate tax bill will become due on the death of Mrs. Gates if she retains the full value of the assets and has not remarried (which would permit her to transfer an unlimited value to her second spouse).

Likewise, over their lifetimes, spouses can make unlimited gifts to a U.S.-citizen spouse without the liability for filing a gift tax return or paying any gift tax. Spouses can make joint gifts to their children and "gift split," thereby getting the advantage of twice the annual gift tax exclusion amount (currently $11,000) for a total gift of $22,000—free of any gift tax liability. (Note: The couple must file a Form 709 gift tax return advising the IRS they have elected to make a split gift.)

Married couples also have the option of filing a tax return either jointly or "married, filing separately" by April 15 each year.

Miscellaneous Other Rights Enjoyed by Married Couples

Common Law Marriage

In the states that still recognize common law marriage, even couples who don't participate in a wedding ceremony may end up with legal obligations related to their union. However, a common law marriage is not created simply by living together—you must intend to be married and hold yourselves out to the world as a married couple. The time period the couple has been together is not the only determining factor—other facts that must be present to have a common law marriage include the following:

1) You must be a heterosexual couple who lives together;
2) You must live in a state that recognizes common law marriage;
3) You must have lived together for a significant length of time—the time may vary from state to state; and
4) You must hold yourself out to the public and your community as a married couple.

If a common law marriage is validated, the spouses receive

the rights, privileges and obligations of the married status under the law. This will include elective share and/or intestacy protections for surviving spouses. The downside of a common law marriage is that if you want to end your relationship, you must divorce, just as a married couple is required to do.

If you live in a common law marriage state and you don't want the law to recognize your relationship as a common law marriage, you should consider signing a written statement making it clear you don't want your relationship interpreted in this way.

---

15 States that Recognize Common Law Marriage

1) Alabama
2) Colorado
3) Georgia (if created before 1/1/1997)
4) Idaho (if created before 1/1/1996)
5) Iowa
6) Kansas
7) Montana
8) New Hampshire (for inheritance purposes only)
9) Ohio (if created before 10/10/1991)
10) Oklahoma
11) Pennsylvania
12) Rhode Island
13) South Carolina
14) Texas
15) Utah

The District of Columbia also recognizes common law marriage.

Loss of Consortium

Loss of consortium is usually defined as the inability of one's spouse to have normal marital relations. This is another way of saying they've been deprived of the right of sexual intercourse, although it can include care, companionship and affection between spouses whether or not there is a decrease or change in sexual activity.

Loss of consortium allows an uninjured spouse the right to join an injured spouse's lawsuit and claim the value of this loss—a value that is often speculative, but can be awarded by the judge or jury if they are sufficiently impressed by the evidence indicating the loss or deprivation.

There have been efforts in some states to extend loss of consortium to same-sex partners and couples who are not married but in a permanent relationship. So far these efforts have been unsuccessful, and there is currently no recovery for loss of consortium by the injured party or the life alliance partner.

Intentional Infliction of Emotional Distress/ Wrongful Death

Like loss of consortium claims, a suit for the intentional infliction of emotional distress or wrongful death is usually reserved for married couples or family members. Life alliance partners generally will not have any claim for compensation if a partner is emotionally injured or killed.

Spousal Privileges

There are two spousal privileges in the eyes of the law. The spousal *testimonial* privilege provides that a spouse may not be compelled to testify against a spouse who is a defendant in a criminal case. A second privilege involves *confidential communications* between spouses and will apply in both civil and criminal cases. Some jurisdictions have both privileges, while others have only one.

The spousal testimonial privilege is sometimes known as the anti-marital fact privilege. The modern justification for this spousal privilege against adverse testimony is its perceived role in fostering the harmony and sanctity of the marriage relationship.[9] This type of privilege is only available in criminal cases, not civil. It only applies to situations arising after the marriage, not to facts that occurred prior to the marriage.

The confidential communications privilege applies in both criminal and civil cases and, again, is designed to promote marital harmony and discourse. It applies only to communications that were intended to be confidential, and the privilege may not apply to conduct, only communications, depending on the jurisdiction.

Liability for Spouse's Debt

Generally, a spouse is not liable for the debts of his or her spouse, although some states make an exception for debts for purchases of household items that are bought for the family and used by the family (Minnesota). You, may however, become responsible for the debts of your spouse if you sign an agreement or contract assuming this responsibility. A credit card agreement is one example of an agreement where both spouses may be liable for a debt. However, if your spouse is unable to control his or her spending, a joint owner of the account has the right to close the account by giving written notice to the credit card company. You will still be liable for any debts created prior to the written notice to close the account.

Liability for Medical Needs

Years ago, a husband was responsible for the medical needs of his wife, but a wife was not responsible for the medical needs of her husband. Today, depending on the jurisdiction, if you are living with your spouse, you may be responsible for the medical needs of your spouse. In Florida, neither a husband nor a wife is responsible for the medical needs of their spouse.

The obligation of one spouse for another in terms of medical debt can have a dramatic impact on families that have significant medical care costs after the death of a spouse or are faced with placing a spouse in a nursing home facility and need the benefits of Medicaid or other government programs.

Family Medical Leave Act (FMLA)

The FMLA requires "covered employers" to provide "eligible employees" up to a total of 12 workweeks of unpaid leave during any 12-month period for one or more of the following reasons:

1) for the birth and care of the newborn child of the employee;

2) for placement with the employee of a son or daughter for adoption or foster care;

3) to care for an immediate family member (spouse, child, or parent) with a serious health condition; or

4) to take medical leave when the employee is unable to work because of a serious health condition.

Generally a "covered employer" is one that employs fifty (50) or more people; and an "eligible employee" is one who:

1) has been employed by the employer for at least twelve months; and

2) has been employed for at least 1,250 hours of service during the twelve-month period immediately preceding the commencement of the leave.

Healthcare Rules/Guardianship

If an individual fails to nominate or empower an agent, the laws of most states make provisions for the appointment of a healthcare surrogate in the event the affected individual is unable to make healthcare decisions for themselves. These laws generally favor spouses and children, and thereafter close family members who are related by blood or marriage. Only after all family relations have been exhausted do these state statutes consider the appointment of a close friend, such as a life alliance partner. The same is true for guardianship proceedings where an incapacitated individual is appointed a guardian by the court. Family members are always given priority before close friends or unmarried partners.

The courts will generally honor the agents named in an individual's healthcare proxies and guardian nomination directives unless evidence is presented to show that this appointment is not appropriate.

Premarital Agreements

A premarital agreement is a written agreement between individuals intending to be married to outline their property rights and responsibilities in the event the marriage is dissolved. It allows the modification of the contract imposed by state marital law. Ownership of property can be established, as well as support obligations in the event of divorce. Twenty-seven (27) states have adopted the Uniform Premarital Agreement Act (the "Act") to allow couples to make written contracts prior to marriage outlining ownership, management and control of property; disposition of property at separation, divorce and death; alimony; wills; and life insurance benefits. The states that haven't adopted the Act have state premarital laws that may differ from the Act in insignificant ways. The one thing the Act prohibits in all instances is the advance determination of child support issues, which are reserved to the discretion of the court. Generally, child support is the child's right and cannot be contracted away by the parents.

Premarital agreements are routinely recognized by courts when the relationship ends, unless one person can demonstrate that the premarital agreement is likely to promote divorce, was signed with the intention of divorcing or was unfairly entered into. Couples contemplating a premarital agreement should each engage the services of separate legal professionals, make a full disclosure of all assets and sign the agreement at least thirty (30) days before the marriage. These steps don't guarantee the success of a premarital agreement but can provide evidence that the parties were fully informed and their rights properly represented. The 30-day time frame is important to avoid a claim of undue influence or duress. Agreements presented for signature without legal representation the night before the wedding have a significantly lower likelihood of success than one which is contemplated well in advance and where both parties have adequate legal representation.

Adoption

All states recognize adoption by married couples or by a step-parent. Some states, however, do not recognize adoption by same-sex couples. In Florida, all gay people are prohibited from adopting children.

Summary

Marriage provides a bundle of rights that life alliance partners do not get automatically. Therefore, it is important for life alliance partners to carefully examine their relationship to determine the bundle of rights they might like to have, and then seek professional advice to determine whether these rights can be obtained through other means.

There are a number of factors to consider in the arena of disability planning. Chapter 4 outlines some of these factors. ♥

Chapter 4

In Sickness and In Health

*I*t is sometimes said that our problem isn't dying too soon, but living too long. This statement points squarely at the issue of disability. In an estate planning environment, when we talk about disability planning we are generally referring to a mental disability rather than a physical disability. If you were to become physically disabled, the likelihood is that you could still manage your financial affairs and make your own medical care decisions. In the event of mental disability, however, you may not be able to make either financial decisions or health care decisions. In this event, it is imperative and even critical that you have proper legal directives in place to clearly state your preference regarding the selection of your agents or surrogates to make your decisions for you.

In late 2003, the national news reported an ongoing battle between parents of a young Florida woman, Terri Schiavo, and her husband-legal guardian. Terri has been in a coma since 1990 and sustained through artificial means since that time. The husband said his wife would never have wanted to be sustained this way. Her parents said she would have wanted to live and, in fact, has some brain activity that warrants sustaining her.

These families, no doubt, have spent countless hours of heartache and soul searching in their attempt to do the right thing. They have spent countless sums for legal fees to have their perspective adopted by the courts. The medical experts have offered opinions about her medical status. The courts have struggled to determine what they are permitted to do under the law. We, as on on-looking public, might also have strong opinions about what should be done.

Nowhere in this picture is a clear written statement from the young woman about whether or not she would like her life artificially prolonged under such conditions. And yet, part of the tragedy is that she had it within her power to express her wishes in the unlikely chance that just such a medical event might occur. Had she executed appropriate legal directives outlining her wishes, the battle between her parents and her husband could have been averted under most circumstances. At the very least, the courts would have had some indication of her own intent.

Most people think estate planning only involves how their "stuff" is distributed when they die. Many, particularly younger people, don't get around to executing these disability directives because the chance of needing them seems slight. Good estate planning involves planning for potential periods of disability before death. As the tragedy of Terri Schiavo and her family shows, disability can sometimes be worse than death for all involved.

The State's Default Plan

Most state statutes provide guidance in addressing mental disability issues. The guidance involves determining when a person is mentally incapacitated, who is authorized to act for them and the scope of the authorization. In general, the state laws will require the decision makers to look first to a named guardian appointed by the court; then to a spouse, if any; then to adult children; then to parents; then to adult relatives; and finally, somewhere further down the line, to close friends. For unmarried individuals, this close friend—your life alliance partner—is the last on the list. This area is ripe for controversy, especially if your life alliance partner and your family don't enjoy a close relationship.

The state laws will appoint someone to take care of you and your financial affairs if you are disabled and have no legal directives in place for this possibility. The person appointed is the "guardian," and the person the guardian is responsible for is called the "ward." There are other details to the state default plan that will be discussed more fully in the section under Guardianship in this chapter.

Avoiding the State's Default Plan

There are a number of legal directives you can prepare to name agents to handle your medical and financial affairs when you are unable to do so for yourself. Each state has laws regarding the formalities the directives must follow to be considered valid. Although some practitioners might use boilerplate, one-size-fits-all forms, there is actually a lot of variety you can request in your directives to fit your particular needs.

The directives fall into two categories: financial directives and healthcare directives. We discuss financial directives first because it has been our experience that this is one of the most overlooked areas of planning. Most people are familiar with healthcare directives, and many have them. However, we have found that it is not uncommon for clients to mistakenly think that their healthcare proxies authorize their agents to handle their financial affairs. Nothing can be further from the truth.

Financial Directives

Powers of Attorney—Financial

A financial power of attorney is a directive that names the individual(s) you select to manage your financial affairs. Special rules apply to assets controlled by a living trust and are discussed later in the chapter. Agents named in such directives are fiduciaries with a legal duty to act for the benefit of the person who created the power of attorney. The fiduciary must use the highest degree of good faith when acting for the maker. The fiduciary duty doesn't permit the agent to place his own interests above the maker's interests and prevents the agent from self-dealing with the maker's assets.

Despite these standards, financial powers must be carefully drafted to avoid giving too little or too much authority to agents. What may be too much authority for one family might not be enough authority in another family. Therefore, you should have a detailed conversation with your advisor regarding what you want and need to accomplish if you are unable to handle your own financial affairs due to a mental incapacity. Some factors you need to consider when deciding what provisions should be in your directives are the following:

1) ***Durable vs. Not Durable.*** It seems counter-intuitive, but unless a financial power states that it is "durable," it loses its power when the maker becomes mentally incapacitated. Therefore, only a Durable Financial Power of Attorney is useful when planning for mental incapacity.

Some financial institutions can raise objections to honoring the agent's acts under a power of attorney on the grounds that the power is stale. State laws can have specific rules determining whether financial institutions have a legitimate legal basis to challenge older powers of attorney. The irony here is that if the power of attorney is determined to be too old and the maker must execute a new one, and the maker is now incapacitated, the purpose for which the durable power of attorney was created in the first place has been thwarted. In this event, a court-ordered guardianship may be the only solution.

2) ***Immediate vs. Springing.*** A durable power of attorney that is effective immediately has its pros and cons. On the pro side, it is available for use without any hurdles— your named agent can use the power of attorney to act on your behalf as soon as the document is signed. Therefore, if you sign the power of attorney and your named agent needs to act on your behalf immediately, he is authorized to do so.

This can be good news or bad news. We've already said that the good news is that it works now. The bad news is that your agent may use the power of attorney in a way that you are not happy with. We often say that an immediately effective durable power of attorney has the same effect as taking out your checkbook, signing a number of blank checks and handing the checkbook over to your agent. This works great if you have a good relationship with your agent. It may be a concern, however, for those who have to think long and hard in order to name someone they can trust in this capacity.

You might decide that it is better to have a springing power of attorney—one that becomes effective when a particular event occurs—a power that doesn't become effective until you're no longer capable of making your own financial decisions. Again, there is good news and bad news associated with a springing power of attorney. The good news is that you may have increased protections against agents using the power when you are still capable of making your own decisions. The bad news is that now they have to jump through a few hurdles in order to show that the triggering event has occurred. The agent will need to satisfy financial institutions or individuals to whom the power of attorney is presented that you are disabled. How do they do this? Well, they'll probably have to obtain and then present some written documentation of disability.

This is what might happen: Your named agent goes to your bank and presents the springing power of attorney with a written letter from two doctors documenting the mental incapacity of the principal (you—the person who gave the power of attorney). The bank teller, manager or customer relations manager doesn't have the authority to decide whether this evidence is sufficient.

They might then direct the agent to their legal department, generally not located on site and many times not even located in the same state. The legal department will then need an attorney who is familiar with your state law so they can make a determination of the validity of the document. And this will take, oh, say, what do you think—minutes, hours or days? We're betting on the last. As a result, we are not big proponents of the springing power of attorney.

As an alternative, you might consider an immediately effective power of attorney but ask your lawyer if he or she will hold the power of attorney in escrow until your agent can provide proof to your lawyer that you are disabled. Again, this may take longer than you want. It's always a balancing act—complexity versus protection. You and your partner need to decide what works best for your situation.

3)   *Limited vs. General Powers of Attorney.* The role of the durable financial power of attorney is to manage financial assets. Powers of attorney can be limited or they can be general in nature. Limited powers of attorney list the specific category of acts the agent can perform for the maker, like sell real estate and make tax elections.

General powers of attorney allow the agent—the person named by the principal or maker of the power of attorney—to handle essentially all financial transactions on behalf of the principal. General durable financial powers of attorney are generally preferred because we may not always be able to predict the circumstances under which the power of attorney will be required. Boilerplate powers of attorney are generally inadequate when it comes to describing those events for which the power of attorney will be required.

Typical acts that can be authorized under a general power of attorney are the ability to sell or lease a home in the event it becomes necessary to raise funds for your care; the ability to prepare your income taxes; the ability to represent you in a lawsuit for the purpose of bringing the suit or settling an existing suit; and the ability to make gifts on your behalf for Medicaid planning or estate tax planning purposes, just to name a few. Your average off-the-shelf power of attorney does not address all of these concerns. It is recommended that you "plan for the worst and hope for the best, because anything else is just wishful thinking." In the legal world, what can go wrong will. Therefore, your best defense is to have estate planning directives that contemplate the bizarre and unusual.

4) ***Unlimited vs. Limited Gifting (amount & recipients).*** The self-dealing rules governing agents prohibit them from giving the maker's assets to themselves or their family without specific authority in the directive to do so. The power of attorney should clearly state the scope of the gifting authority: unlimited (specific amount or formula) or unlimited. Gifting authority can be a strategy to reduce taxes or for long-term care asset protection.

5) ***Dual Agents vs. Alternate Agents.*** The maker can have two or more agents authorized to act, or have someone

identified as "runner-up" when the initial agent can't serve. Problems can arise when two authorized agents disagree or if third parties require proof of the first agent's inability to serve. Be sure your power of attorney clearly states whether a majority or unanimous decision is required.

6) ***Revoking a Power of Attorney.*** You can revoke a power of attorney any time while you are mentally competent. However, communicating to others that you have revoked your power of attorney can become difficult. To revoke a power of attorney, you need to execute a written revocation and then deliver a copy of the revocation to any financial institutions and third parties who might have relied on the original financial power of attorney.

You should normally file a copy of a power of attorney with a county recorder's office if you want financial institutions to rely on your agent's authority regarding the sale of real estate. In this way, the financial institutions or third parties can inspect the public record to verify that the agent under the power has the authority to perform the sale of the property. If you have filed a power with the recorder's office and you want to revoke the power, you need to file a copy of the revocation with the recorder's office, as well, so third parties are on notice that the power has been revoked.

These considerations should underscore that there is a lot of decision making that goes into drafting a financial power of attorney that meets the specific needs and concerns of an individual. Selection of the agents and the scope of their powers are crucial to achieving your goals and managing your affairs when you are no longer able to do so. Every life alliance couple should have these legal directives.

Healthcare Directives

Healthcare directives authorize agents to make medical decisions for you when you are mentally incapacitated. The directives can have different names in different jurisdictions. The generic names are "healthcare proxy" or "healthcare surrogate." The directives come into play in two separate circumstances:

Heroic or Life-Sustaining Medical Treatment

The directive referred to as a "living will" in many jurisdictions is created to provide written instructions stating whether the maker wants life-sustaining treatment or procedures withheld or withdrawn if they are unable to make informed medical decisions and are in a terminal condition or in a permanently unconscious state. Comfort care, such as pain medication, can be continued if it is to reduce pain, even if they choose not to authorize life-sustaining treatment.

The living will also permits you to specify whether or not you want artificially or technologically supplied food and water. Such treatment may be provided unless you specifically indicate you do not want them.

The living will names the people you want to act as your agents regarding life-sustaining decisions. The agents cannot override your instructions in the living will but it makes sense to discuss your wishes with potential agents to make sure the named agents can make the difficult decisions, if necessary. You should select someone you trust, who understands your wishes regarding the termination of life and will have the emotional fortitude to carry through. We love the story of a friend who said he could never choose his wife for this role because she loved him too much. Instead, he selected his sister, who he says never liked him very much anyway.

A well-drafted living will specifically defines the terms it uses in order to reduce potential dispute over your intended definitions. One example is the use of the word "persistent vegetative state." If you want to continue all forms of life-sustaining treatment, including CPR, you should clearly state your medical preferences in writing. If your agent is authorized to execute a DNR or "do not resuscitate" order, you should say so. If you have particular religious or other concerns about the use of blood transfusions or other matters, you should also clearly state your instructions in this directive.

Durable Healthcare Power of Attorney (Health Care Surrogate)

Situations can occur when you might be unable to communicate for yourself but you don't meet the criteria for invoking a living will. For instance, you might experience a stroke that temporarily makes you unable to speak or makes you mentally incapacitated. In this event, you will need someone to sign medical consent forms and authorize your medical providers regarding your medical care. The directive for this situation is often called a durable healthcare power of attorney or healthcare surrogate.

The purpose of this directive is to identify the agents who are authorized to make most healthcare decisions for you if you lose the capacity to make informed healthcare decisions for yourself. They are generally not effective until you are unable to make your own medical care decisions. The types of decisions that get made with a durable healthcare power of attorney are everyday type medical care decisions, like consent to surgery, consent to treatment, transfer to or from a medical facility, the hiring and firing of nurses, doctors and therapists, and the release of medical information and records.

You can authorize or limit the specific types of healthcare decisions your agent can make for you. For instance, you could authorize the agent to consent to surgical procedures for you but limit the agent's ability to move you to a different healthcare facility. You can include specific directions for your agents regarding healthcare decisions that invoke religious beliefs, such as for blood transfusions or other procedures.

Health Information Portability and Accountability Act (HIPAA)

A durable health care power of attorney has become especially important in light of the newly implemented regulations under the Health Information Portability and Accountability Act (HIPAA) that became effective in June 2003. Under HIPAA, you must name a "personal representative" for the purpose of transacting business on your behalf with your healthcare providers and insurers.

For those of you already familiar with HIPAA, it may have caused you problems. Peggy was unable to obtain a copy of her own contact lens prescription when out of town on business because she had failed to designate such an individual in advance, in writing, at her doctor's office. It didn't matter that she was giving them verbal authorization over the phone. A client with a husband in the hospital in a coma called when she needed to contact the husband's insurance company to discuss his benefits eligibility. The insurance company refused to talk with her because she was not the insured. He was clearly unable to communicate on his own behalf, yet she had not been properly designated as his personal representative. Protect yourself and your life alliance partner to make sure your healthcare power of attorney contains proper instructions to nominate your healthcare surrogate as your personal representative under the provisions of HIPAA.

There is a debate in some legal circles as to whether a separate directive is required to meet the standards required by HIPAA. You should discuss this with your legal advisor to determine whether it makes sense to prepare a separate directive to satisfy potential challenges as to whether your healthcare proxies comply with HIPAA—just to be on the safe side. The separate directive normally will be a statement authorizing the agents named in the healthcare proxies to make decisions consistent with the authority under HIPAA.

Visitation in Healthcare Facilities

Some healthcare facilities restrict visitors to immediate family when a patient is in intensive care or other circumstances where medical circumstances dictate limiting visits. Family is defined by most facilities as next of kin. This could cause unnecessary distress for loved ones of unmarried partners since children of unmarried partners will not be able to visit under these restrictions and the partners themselves may also be barred.

You should include a specific authorization regarding the people who will be permitted to visit you when visitation is normally restricted to next of kin. You should consult with your legal advisor to decide whether this type of authorization should be incorporated in the durable healthcare power of attorney or whether it should be a separate document. If the directive is a separate document, you should make sure that it complies with the same legal formalities as the durable health-care power of attorney. This directive should also specify that it is "durable" to ensure that it retains its legal authority during any period in which you have lost mental capacity.

Legal Formalities

State laws on healthcare proxies require they be executed with certain legal formalities. The formalities can differ from state to state. They should be signed before a notary or before two disinterested witnesses who are present when you sign your name. The following people are generally ineligible to be witnesses to these proxies: anyone who is related to you by blood, marriage or adoption; your attorney-in-fact (someone with a financial power of attorney); and your doctor or the administrator of any nursing home in which you are receiving care. Copies of the properly executed forms are as good as an original.

If you are a "snow bird" who regularly travels to another state, it is advisable that you make sure your directives comply with the standards of that state as well as your home state.

Although the full faith and credit principles of the U.S. Constitution should permit a document properly drafted in your home state to be honored in other states, it makes sense to reduce the chance that a healthcare provider could challenge the legality of a directive based on a technicality.

Where to Keep Your Healthcare Proxies

It is important to understand that these proxies are only useful if they are available to your agents and healthcare providers in a medical emergency. You should provide a copy to each agent you have named and to your doctors. You should also have one readily available for yourself, particularly if you travel.

For a small subscription fee, you can file your proxies with a repository company and your forms can be available via fax to healthcare providers worldwide, 24/7. The repository gives you a wallet card to keep with your insurance card. The wallet card has instructions on how to obtain the forms. For more information you can contact www.docubank.com.

Guardianship

During a period of mental incapacity, someone must pay your bills and make financial decisions to take care of you, your family and other obligations. If you own accounts jointly, the joint owner can continue to use those accounts. But if a life alliance partner isn't named on all accounts, financial institutions can demand that you show proof of your authority to act. The financial directives discussed previously can be that proof.

If you don't have the proper legal directives or if they don't cover a particular situation, you might need to get a court order showing you have legal authority to act for the disabled person. The process of getting this authority is called a "guardianship" proceeding and is controlled by the state probate laws. This is why it is sometimes referred to as "living probate"—the probate laws apply while you are living.

Guardianship proceedings involve three factors: 1) Determination of mental incapacity; 2) Giving of authority over the ward and/or the ward's affairs; 3) Accounting to the court regarding the ward's affairs.

First, guardianship requires that you produce medical evidence of the person's mental incapacity. The statute will normally require that the level of proof required to prove that a person has lost his mental capacity must be "clear and convincing" evidence or some other appropriate level. The courts are reluctant to take away a person's autonomy. Therefore, the level of proof is sufficiently high to confine court intervention to serious situations.

Second, the court will then determine who should be appointed the guardian of the incapacitated person. The hierarchy of state-sanctioned candidates for guardians is governed by statute. You can nominate a guardian for yourself as discussed below, but the court is not bound by the nomination.

The court might divide the authority "over the person" and "over the estate" of the incapacitated ward. This means that a family member might be named as the guardian over the physical well-being of the ward, but an accountant or professional guardian might be named to handle the financial affairs. This is likely to occur where the court has some concern that a family member lacks sophistication or is at risk to exploit the ward or be exploited if placed in charge of the ward's finances.

Third, regular accounting reports must be given to the court to permit it to supervise the guardian's activities. Expenditures from the ward's assets must comply with specific standards and the court will review all accounts on a regular basis— usually bi-annually or annually. Failure to comply with the standards required by the court can be grounds for removal of the guardian.

The guardian can normally receive reasonable compensation for handling the ward's affairs. Non-family members who are named as guardians are usually required to secure a bond (like an insurance policy) to cover losses to the ward's financial accounts due the guardian's fault or neglect.

If the ward regains mental capacity, the ward will need to produce medical proof of this fact and convince the court to return authority to the ward to handle his own affairs.

Pre-Need Guardian Declaration Directive

A pre-need guardian declaration is a directive that states your desires for the selection of a guardian of the person or guardian of the property in the event your other disability directives are ineffective or absent and there is an incapacity proceeding to determine your capacity. State statutes will generally favor family members over life alliance partners unless you make your selection known.

A pre-need guardian directive is normally what we refer to as "a sweater in a suitcase." We don't generally need it at the time it is created, but like that extra sweater we pack when we take a trip where the weather can be uncertain, it sure is nice to have it when we need it. The pre-need guardian declaration stands by and is not used unless and until there is a guardianship proceeding pending.

If you are nominating your life alliance partner as your guardian of choice, it may be important to clearly state the long-term committed nature of your relationship. This is necessary to make it clear to the judge why this selection is important.

Other General Issues Regarding Disability

In the event of a disability, unmarried partners face a number of hurdles that may not be present for their married counterparts. Spouses always have a preference as healthcare surrogates and agents, and as guardians. The rules for applying for and receiving disability compensation favor married couples. A life alliance partner cannot make a disability claim utilizing the earning history of a partner, as is possible with a spouse. Therefore, life alliance partners must make specific financial plans and arrangements to address the concerns that may arise in the event one of the partners becomes disabled and is not able to work. The same is true after retirement if one of the partners must enter a nursing home—the rules do not necessarily favor unmarried couples. For any type of government eligibility program, the rules for life alliance partners are inevitably the rules that apply to single individuals. In some instances, this can be an advantage or it can be a disadvantage. If you live in a spousal support state, marriage may actually be a disadvantage if one party needs to qualify for Medicaid but the family assets exceed the limitations for eligibility.

What happens if both life alliance partners are living in a retirement facility and one of them requires around-the-clock assisted care? Unlike married couples, it may not be possible for life alliance partners to remain together; and the result is separation of the partners. If staying together is important to you, clearly state this requirement in your planning. Make it known that separation is only acceptable as a last resort.

Trusts—Financial and Healthcare Directives on Steroids

The prior sections illustrate the potential dangers a family faces when a family member becomes mentally incapacitated. This is particularly important since insurance statistics show that we have a greater likelihood of becoming disabled at a young age than of dying prematurely.

Trusts are normally discussed in terms of "death planning," and Chapter 5 explains many of the advantages trusts hold for avoiding some of the threats to our loved ones and their financial support when we die. Often, what is not discussed is the power trusts offer in the context of disability planning.

Well-designed trusts have the potential to permit you to avoid guardianship proceedings, to keep your healthcare and financial matters private, and to permit you the ability to name those you love and have confidence in to manage your affairs for you when you cannot do so for yourself. For life alliance partners this can be of particular concern because of the inherent biases favoring next of kin over partners regarding health and financial powers of attorney.

A trust can allow you the flexibility of naming a life alliance partner and others you trust to a disability panel to determine if and when you are mentally incapacitated. For this concept to make sense, you have to think about the process. There are a couple of ways a person can be declared mentally disabled. One way is a voluntary designation of disability. One morning you simply wake up, decide you are no longer capable of managing your own financial affairs and making your own health care decisions, and you resign as trustee of your trust in favor of your designated successor trustee. Easy to say, harder to do in practice. It is the rare individual who recognizes he no longer has the mental capacity to make his own decisions. Rather, the reality is that most people who have lost their mental faculties have no idea they are not operating on all cylinders and proceed through life as if everything is fine.

This is where the creation and selection of a disability panel, empowered under the terms of a trust, becomes important. It is your opportunity to construct a panel of individuals you trust to make difficult decisions regarding your mental disability. Therefore, it is critical that, at a time when you are actually going to be in disagreement with these people, you trust their judgment enough to make this difficult decision for you.

Generally, it is recommended that you consider some combination of both medical personnel and family or friends. You should include someone from the medical community to make sure you are getting a competent evaluation of all the factors that might result in a mental disability determination. Typically, these medical representatives may include your primary care physician and a specialist recommended by your primary care physician and approved by your life alliance partner or trusted family member. In these days of HMOs, some people do not feel comfortable naming their primary care physician as part of their disability panel because they don't feel they enjoy the type of close, personal relationship with this person that will allow the doctor to make an informed decision. You may want to carefully consider whether naming your primary care physician adds complexity to the disability determination process or provides an element of protection. In theory, your primary care physician is the person who maintains custody of your permanent medical history.

The specialist on your panel could be a doctor specializing in the type of mental incapacity you are suffering from. Therefore, the exact identity of this person may not be known, but a description as to the type of physician is included in the trust to ensure their participation on the disability panel. You can instruct that the primary care physician select a physician of appropriate medical specialty and give the right to approve the selection to your life alliance partner or other trusted family member. This gives your life alliance partner a measure of control to determine the medical component that will comprise your disability panel.

There is no limit to the number of individuals you can place on your panel, but carefully consider the possible result when too many committee members are trying to make a decision.

After the disability panel members and appropriate alternates have been identified, it is also important to consider whether their decision should be a unanimous or a majority decision.

The panel's sole responsibility is to decide if you are mentally incapacitated. Thereafter, upon a finding of mental incapacity, the panel plays no role unless they are asked to determine whether you have regained capacity at some point in the future.

Once the disability determination has been made, a different individual or group of individuals assume management responsibility for the trust and must manage the trust assets. The new individual or individuals might actually be some of the same people you named to be on your disability panel. However, they will not be acting in the role of disability panel once the determination is made. They will be acting as "disability trustee," and the scope of their responsibility involves only managing the trust assets for the benefit of the beneficiary—you—according to the instructions you provide in the trust document.

The instructions you provide in your trust for the management of your finances and your personal care during mental disability are very important. Many boilerplate type trusts simply say that, "if two doctors determine the trustmaker is mentally incapacitated, then the successor trustee(s) shall take over the management of the assets." Rarely are boilerplate instructions complete as to how this day-to-day management is to be accomplished. Therefore, your trust instructions need to be complete and specific with regard to how your assets may be spent on your behalf or on behalf of your loved ones (including your pets) when you are no longer directing the actual distribution of assets.

You should consider crafting instructions that specifically identify the individuals, including yourself, who may benefit from the trust assets during disability. These individuals might include your life alliance partner, your dependent children, other family members who may be dependent upon you for their support, such as parents or siblings, and last but not least, your pets. In addition, you should give good instructions regarding your living conditions, lifestyle, access to friends, family and pets and your specific likes and dislikes regarding your continuing care. Remember, you should craft these instructions while you are competent because you may not be able to communicate your wishes and desires regarding your care during a period of mental disability.

Summary

Our personal living trusts give instructions that simply state we would prefer to remain in our homes during any period of mental disability, and only if it becomes impractical or impossible for us to stay in our homes should our partners consider an alternate living arrangement. In the event we must live somewhere other than our home, it is our desire that we live in a place that is consistent with our maximum degree of independence. For both of us, this includes an environment that is pet-friendly and willing to accept at least one, if not all, of our small cats and dogs. It is unlikely we could find a place that would accept horses, but... In addition, our trusts provide that our successor trustees can spend all of our assets, if necessary, to provide for the level of care we have dictated. We also include language to instruct our successor trustee to look for more detailed hand-written instructions with regard to our personal preferences for daily care, such as hair color, make-up, special treats and our own peculiarities. Our successor trustees are also instructed not to pay for care inconsistent with our living will and to seek guidance from our written memorial instructions in the event we die and such arrangements become necessary.

When all is said and done, if you don't leave good disability instructions, your successor disability trustees won't be provided with guidance in order to give you the type of continuing care you desire. In our upcoming book, *A Matter of Trust,* we will describe some of the horror stories associated with boilerplate trusts, poor disability instructions and corporate trustees—a lethal combination that can result in sub-standard care even when there are more than sufficient assets to provide a comfortable lifestyle.

If you choose not to prepare a living trust and instead intend to rely on your last will and testament as your final expression of your wishes in the event of your death, it is wise to ensure that your estate plan include a better-than-average durable financial power of attorney, durable health care power of attorney, living will, anatomical gift declaration and pre-need guardian declaration. Each of these planning directives meets a different need, but all are important to a well-rounded, comprehensive disability plan.

The specifics of the decisions we need to make when planning for what happens when we die are discussed in depth in the next chapter. ♥

Chapter 5

Until Death Do Us Part

Whether you are married or unmarried, when you die, three things occur: 1. Final arrangements for your physical remains are completed; 2. Your estate is settled or administered; and 3. Your loved ones carry on life without you. The legacy you leave for them will consist of more than just tangible things. If you plan ahead with appropriate legal directives to authorize your final wishes and estate matters, the unintended outcomes your loved ones might face with legal issues will be reduced. If you fail to plan ahead, your loved ones can be the unfortunate victims of legal processes that dictate outcomes you would not choose for them.

A long-standing statistic reveals that more than half the population (married or unmarried) does not have even basic wills or other legal directives in place to direct their affairs at disability or death. More than half of this segment have college degrees. This means that even educated people have failed to protect themselves with basic estate planning directives.

Some statistics report that out of the people who do have wills, more than 40% of the wills are ten years old or older. As discussed in prior chapters, if you die without a will, state laws will dictate what your loved ones are entitled to receive. If your will is old and out of date when you die, it may not accurately reflect your wishes. Your personal representative will be required to follow your written instructions you have left behind.

As discussed previously, the survivor of a married couple has many protections when a partner dies—even when a deceased spouse failed to execute appropriate legal directives. Unmarried partners are particularly vulnerable to bad outcomes if they fail to do planning. Remember, even in jurisdictions that have extended rights to unmarried partners, the Defense of Marriage Act (DOMA)—a federal law—says "married" is defined as between a man and a woman. Until such time that the conflict between DOMA and the states' provisions are resolved in the courts, same-sex partners should conclude that state probate codes will not extend the rights of inheritance to unmarried partners.

We all need to plan for the time when we will die. Life alliance partners must pay particular attention to the legal directives we have in place to protect our loved ones and ease the process for the survivor after we are gone. The following highlights some areas that require particular attention for life alliance partners.

Final Arrangements

A topic that doesn't receive much attention in most discussions on estate planning is what to do with the deceased person's remains. The likely explanation for this omission is that married couples generally have the right to handle this matter privately. Some states have statutes that provide for who has priority to make these decisions if the deceased person has failed to make arrangements. Surviving spouses and next of kin have priority on this list. Unmarried partners are not on the list. This means that, in the eyes of the law, family members will have greater priority than the surviving life alliance partner even if the family has been estranged from the deceased. If the family and surviving partner disagree, the law could legitimately support the family over the surviving life alliance partner regarding the remains.

Similar problems can arise about the funeral arrangements. Without explicit instructions that authorize your partner to carry out your directions, family members will have a higher authority to make these decisions, and can even exclude your partner from the funeral service.

You can make written instructions setting forth your wishes for disposition of your remains when you die. If you fail to do so, state law has provisions listing, in order of priority, those who are authorized to make decisions regarding your remains. Your instructions regarding disposition of your remains and funeral arrangements should set forth your wishes on the following:

- Cremation, burial or donation to science
- If you want a funeral, include details as to whether you want a viewing; the type and cost of a casket; flowers or donations to charities in lieu of flowers
- Religious or other type of service; whether you want special music or a reading you would like included in the service
- Obituary, or death notices including how you want your partner listed as a survivor
- Any other details, including parting words, you would like to include regarding your final arrangements

Your memorial letter of instruction is called a "precatory" letter and is not binding, but will provide guidance to your partner and family members. If you have concerns that your wishes might not be followed, either due to financial reasons or because family members who are hostile to your partner might intervene, you should consider making pre-paid funeral arrangements. Pre-paid funerals can include every detail you want for your final arrangements. Family members are less likely to dispute arrangements if they don't bear the financial responsibility for them. However, be aware that most pre-paid plans are not transferable to other states if you move. You should thoroughly explore your options and have the contract for funeral services reviewed by a legal professional.

If you decide not to make pre-paid funeral arrangements, you should have some idea about how your final arrangements will be paid for. Insurance is the traditional mechanism most people use to cover funeral costs, and it is sometimes available through your employer as a work-related benefit. Unmarried individuals who cannot get such benefits at work will have to make other financial arrangements to have their wishes followed.

Administering Your Estate

Passing on Your 'Stuff'

As the old saying goes, "You can't take it with you." When we die, the "stuff" we own gets passed on to survivors. The generic term for this process is "estate settlement" or "estate administration." When we settle an estate, we will transfer title to our stuff to others in basically three ways:

- Probate
- Operation of law
- Contract

The method of transfer and the consequences of the transfer depend on a number of factors. The factors that life alliance partners share with married couples are as follows:

- How title to assets is held
- What legal directives are in place to direct the assets at death
- The total value of the deceased person's estate

Factors unique to life alliance partners:

- The amount(s) each partner contributed to acquire the asset
- The amount(s) each partner gave to others during life (in other words, the total gifts over the annual gift exclusions during their lifetime)

An effective estate plan will coordinate these factors with the specific needs and goals of the partners. Obviously, boilerplate and do-it-yourself wills and other legal directives will not produce a good result for the unique needs of unmarried couples.

Title Controls

How title to assets is held and how title affects transfers of assets is one of the most misunderstood areas for non-lawyers facing estate planning decisions. Few people realize that every time they open a bank or brokerage account, complete a beneficiary designation form or execute a deed, they are engaging in estate planning, of sorts.

Most people think of estate planning as creating a will or a trust. They also don't realize that a will or a trust is useless if they own title to property as joint tenants with rights of survivorship (JTROS or JTWROS) with another person .

A lot of estate planning involves creating a combination of types of ownership to accomplish your estate planning goals. Consequently, it is important to understand the different categories of title, and that each specific category of title controls which mechanism is used to transfer assets at death. Without this understanding, you might not have the proper scope of legal directives to achieve your goals. Your estate planning goals can be anything from minimizing the delay and expense of administration or estate taxes to avoiding probate or providing asset protection for survivors among a number of other worthy estate planning objectives.

The basic rules regarding how assets are transferred are the same for both married and unmarried couples. It is just that state rules build in safety nets for married partners and their children to make sure they are not disinherited accidentally. Unmarried partners have no automatic safety nets. It is essential that unmarried partners create their own safety nets and ensure that their wishes will be followed.

Understanding the rules that control transfers at death is easiest if you remember that each category of ownership has an "instruction sheet" for the disposition of the asset. The instruction sheet might be a will, a beneficiary designation or contract terms.

Probate

Probate is a state-authorized court process to settle the deceased person's final debts and to formally pass legal title to property from the deceased person's name to others. A will is the instruction sheet for property titled in a person's individual name. If there is no will, or if it is invalid for some reason, the probate process will follow the probate law rules for people who have died intestate. Both methods are called probate.

A person who makes a will is called the testator or testatrix. A person who does not have a valid will is said to have died intestate and intestate succession is the term to describe the state probate laws list the categories of next of kin who stand in line to receive probate property where the deceased died without a valid will.

The probate process *only* controls property in a person's individual name. The probate process does *not* control property that is held as joint tenants with survivorship rights, property that passes with beneficiary designations or property that has been titled in the name of a trust. However, if there is a flaw in any of these ownership categories, the probate process might be required to pass title of the asset because the original "instructions" for that asset can no longer be followed. It is also important to note that joint title forms of ownership that do *not* include appropriate survivorship language are controlled by the probate process.

There are essentially three steps in the probate process. The first is to identify and gather all of the decedent's assets that are owned in the decedent's individual name. The second is to identify and pay all of the decedent's creditors within a statutorily prescribed time frame. Third, beneficiaries are clearly identified, either through the decedent's will or by the rules of intestate succession and the remaining assets are distributed to the identified beneficiaries.

The term "probate estate" refers to the assets that are controlled by the probate process. The probate estate will not include property that does not require the probate process to pass title to others. The probate estate is not the same thing as the taxable estate for estate tax purposes.

Some of the disadvantages of probate you should consider in your decision-making are as follows:

- Probate is a public proceeding. This means the nature and extent of the probate assets can be scrutinized by anyone who cares to look up the record.

- The probate process requires filing fees, legal costs, appraiser fees for real estate and special types of assets and accounting fees. These fees can add up to sizeable amounts. (Note: some or most of these fees may be required even if probate is avoided.)

- If a trust is created in the will, called a testamentary trust, there may be additional costs to the estate for the ongoing administration of these trusts pursuant to the instructions in the will.

- The probate process can be lengthy, depending on the nature of the probate assets. Beneficiaries under the will generally do not gain access to the assets while the process is pending. However, most probate laws give surviving spouses access to limited sums to live on while the probate process is pending. There is currently no comparable provision for unmarried partners to receive a similar allowance while the probate is pending. Unmarried partners are treated no differently than single beneficiaries in the eyes of the law.

- Disgruntled heirs (blood relatives) can challenge a will before the probate judge and, perhaps, change some of the distributions set forth in the will.

The probate process has some advantages: One advantage is that the decedent's creditors have to present their claims to the decedent's estate within specified time frames or forego payment. Another advantage is, ironically, one of its disadvantages—the fact that the process is public. This means that it is subject to scrutiny by others, a fact that may make it more difficult for mishandling of the probate estate assets. Finally, it is a court-supervised process that must follow procedures that can impose a degree of orderliness and predictability to the process.

Even if life alliance partners prefer to avoid the probate process, it is a good idea for them to have wills in place anyway. Wills can act as a safety net if there is a defect in another transfer mechanism or if the decedent dies with an unexpected asset in their own name. This can occur if they receive an inheritance from a family member and die shortly thereafter. The will controls those assets rather than requiring application of the intestate succession probate rules. Remember, the intestate succession rules in most states will not give inheritance rights to life alliance partners.

Wills

Wills must be executed with certain legal formalities to be considered valid. Each state decides what formalities must be followed. In general, most states require that the maker of a will have legal capacity (be competent), be of legal age (at least eighteen years old), and that the will was executed of the maker's free and intentional act. You must follow the rules of the state in which you reside at the time the will is executed.

Most states require that the will be written and signed by the maker of the will before one or more witnesses. Handwritten wills, called holographic wills, are permitted in many states and may not need to be witnessed but must meet other standards to be considered valid. Each state will have its own requirements for a holographic will to be considered valid. We know of one instance where a will that was written on a piece of notebook paper in the hospital and witnessed was validly admitted for probate purposes. We don't generally, however, recommend do-it-yourself wills.

Wills don't have to follow a particular format, but they usually do. The first paragraph normally recites the essential elements about the maker of the will being of legal age and sound mind, and how the making of the will was his own free act. The next paragraph in a will normally authorizes payment of the maker's debts, the costs of administration and taxes from his estate after death. The next paragraph may direct the distribution of personal property and the following paragraph will generally direct the remainder of the estate to whomever he wants. This is normally referred to as the "residuary estate" clause because it directs the balance (the residuary) of the estate after paying taxes and debts.

The will should nominate someone to act as the personal representative of the estate. This person is normally called the executor (male) or executrix (female) and the clause can specify whether they must post a bond and whether they are entitled to collect a fee for performing their duties as the personal representative. A bond is like an insurance policy to protect the estate from losses caused by the personal representative if he or she fails to properly carry out his or her duties.

If minor children are involved, the will should contain a clause nominating a guardian and alternates for the children and other provisions, such as a trust created under the will for taking care of the children until they reach the age of majority or some other specified age. A trust created under the will is called a "testamentary trust." This is different from a revocable living trust (RLT) because, unlike an RLT, a testamentary trust must undergo the probate process because it is established in the will.

A detailed discussion of the requirements for executing a will is beyond the scope of this book. However, it is important to note that life alliance partners should consult an attorney to have their wills prepared in order to be confident that the will meets the standards required in their state. Partners should never rely on do-it-yourself forms available through the Internet or in self-help books. This is fool-hardy for most married couples to do, but at least they have the intestate rules that are better than nothing. Unmarried partners do not currently have intestate rules that favor their relationship.

Operation Of Law

States can create categories of property ownership that, by the terms of the state law, automatically give ownership of the property to the surviving owners at the death of an owner. These types of ownership that either are created by the common law of a state or are codified by state statute. For example, tenancy by the entirety (TBE) is a type of survivorship ownership that is limited to married couples. Probate is not required to determine who receives the property at the owner's death.

Assets Held Jointly With Others

People can own assets with others as tenants in common (TC or TIC) and as joint tenants with rights of survivorship (JTROS or JTWROS). Most people prefer the JTROS form of ownership but sometimes make a mistake, and do not include the required "survivorship" language when executing a deed. Therefore, they think they have JTROS when they actually have created TC ownership. The difference determines whether they need probate to pass title at death, among other things.

Tenants in Common (TC or TIC)

At death, a person's interest in TC assets is controlled by a person's will since they own a specified percentage of the asset and can convey that interest to others during life and at death. The beneficiary(ies) under the will becomes the joint owner of the asset with the other joint owners. There is no built-in survivorship language in a TC owned asset.

Joint Tenants with Rights of Survivorship (JTROS or JTWROS)

This form of property ownership is probably one of the most common examples of the operation of law principles. It is popular because it is easy to create and inexpensive. Many people choose this type of ownership because it avoids probate and appears to create a fair division of assets between couples, married or not. For many life alliance partners, it symbolizes their commitment and seems to protect their mutual interests in each other's property. However, these so-called advantages can obscure some of the less desirable qualities of JTROS, such as:

- The asset is available to the creditors of both joint owners. Joint ownership with rights of survivorship property is subject to the creditors of either owner. If one of the joint owners has liabilities from a serious accident, a failed business or for some other reason, the jointly held property could be attached to cover the joint owner's debts. This is one of the primary reasons joint ownership of property is not recommended for even married individuals.

- A taxable gift can be triggered if unmarried owners contribute unequal amounts to the cost of acquiring the asset. When a couple, married or unmarried, buys property and creates a JTROS deed, in the eyes of the IRS there is a gift to any partner who did not contribute equally toward the cost of acquiring the property.

- For married couples, this gift is not a problem due to the unlimited gifts permitted between married couples. For unmarried couples, unintended gift taxes can be triggered. If the portion of the property titled to the non-contributing partner exceeds the annual gift exclusion limit of $11,000, there will be an obligation on the donor partner to file a gift tax return and report the gift to the IRS. The effect of these lifetime gifts in excess of the annual exclusion limit is to reduce the amount a person can leave at the time of death without an estate tax obligation.

- The entire value of the asset will be included in the estate (for purposes of calculating the federal gross estate tax) of the first owner to die unless the survivor can produce proof of his or her contributions to the property or other proof as to why less than the full amount should be included. The survivor might want to show less than full ownership by the deceased owner in order to reduce the federal estate tax and state estate tax, if any.

- Structuring financial accounts as joint tenants with rights of survivorship makes the account available to all joint owners and any partner can legally withdraw all of the account funds without the permission of the other owners. Indeed, one of the first instructions divorce attorneys normally give their clients is to immediately remove all assets from joint accounts to obtain control over the funds and have the upper hand in negotiations thereafter. Consequently, in the context of unmarried partners, you should always carefully consider whether joint ownership with rights of survivorship is prudent. Unmarried partners will not have many of the protections the domestic relations courts provide to divorcing partners.

- There can be income tax consequences to unmarried couples who own property as joint tenants with rights of survivorship. The income tax consequences involve capital gains on property. The cost to acquire a piece of property or an asset is called the "basis." If property is later sold or transferred, the capital gain (or loss) is calculated on the difference between the basis and the sale price or its fair market value on the date of transfer.

- When a property transfers at the death of the owner, the tax basis of the property is the fair market value of the property on the date-of-death even if the transfer is actually finalized later. In tax terminology, this is called a "step-up in basis" which means that the recipient of the property acquires a basis in the property equal to the fair market value of the property on the date of the owner's death. Then, when the property is sold, the capital gain is the difference between the value on the date-of-death and the amount for which the property was sold. The recipient isn't required to use the value of the property when the property owner originally acquired the property. Obviously, this can save large sums of money in capital gains taxes.

The most recent federal estate tax laws have modified the rules on step-up in basis at death, and there is some debate whether these rules will remain in place. Therefore, it will be important for a couple, married or unmarried, to consult with appropriate advisors if their assets are sizeable to be sure they understand the tax consequences of transferring their estates at death.

Joint owners who receive property as a result of rights of survivorship only receive a percentage of the step-up in basis. This percentage correlates with the percentage of their contribution to acquire the property. Married couples are presumed to have contributed 50% each. One hundred percent (100%) of a person's joint property will be included in the estate of the first of the unmarried partners to die unless the partners can show the actual percentage they contributed to acquire the property.

- A joint owner requires consent of the other owner to sell property held as JTROS during life (this can be a good thing as well—read the section on disadvantages for contract assets below).

- There is no mechanism to hold JTROS property in trust for the benefit of a disabled survivor partner. If the survivor tenant is in a nursing home at the time the other owner passes away, the value of the property might make the survivor ineligible for public benefits that are based on financial need.

- Joint ownership with rights of survivorship does not work well in the event of the simultaneous deaths of partners since the property will be included in the estate of both partners. The second partner will not have time to make alternative plans. In Florida, the law presumes that if all of the joint tenants with right of survivorship die simultaneously, or it is impossible to determine the order of death, each individual is deemed to have owned 50% of the property in their individual name. As a result, the property will thereafter be distributed pursuant to the deceased's will or state laws of intestacy.

- Federal and state estate taxes might be due at the death of the first owner and the estate might not have sufficient liquid assets to cover them. In addition to gift and estate tax consequences, if a partner, either married or unmarried, is not a U.S. citizen the rules for gift and inheritance taxes may vary. In some states, there may also be a state inheritance or estate tax at the time of death.

- "He who lives last, controls." Or put another way, "He who lives the longest wins." In any event, the surviving partner can decide who gets the asset once it is transferred to the survivor's name on the death of the first partner—regardless of the original understanding of the joint owner partners. Therefore, there is no guarantee the property will go to the people originally agreed upon between the partners.

   This can hold particular importance to partners who want to provide for children from prior relationships after the demise of the second partner or where there are concerns that the survivor-joint owner might be vulnerable to exploitation in subsequent relationships.

   We have both seen examples where parents in a second relationship have assured their respective children from prior relationships that they will be provided for in the event of their parents' death. In one case, however, at the husband's death it was discovered that the bulk of the assets were owned as joint tenants with rights of survivorship with the wife, or the wife was named as the beneficiary of life insurance and retirement plans. As a result, the wife became the sole owner of 100% of the property and she was free to use this property during her lifetime and then to distribute it at the time of her death as she might choose. She has made it clear to her husband's children that they are not included in her estate plan. This is an all too common scenario that is repeated daily upon the death of a spouse in a second or more marriage situation.

Transfer on Death Deeds (TOD) or Deeds with a Retained Life Estate or Remainder

These deeds to real estate are individually owned titles with a survivorship or remainder feature. The asset remains in the individual name of the owner but it is *not* controlled by a will or the probate process because the deed has a built-in survivorship provision that directs who gets the property at the owner's death.

This type of deed is easy to create and inexpensive. The survivor merely produces proof of the death of the owner, and an affidavit is generally filed with the county recorder's office to create a paper trail showing how and why title was transferred.

TOD assets do not have all of the disadvantages that JTROS property have in terms of potential gift tax issues or being subject to a joint owner's control or creditor's control. Some disadvantages of TOD are as follows:

- The entire value of the asset is included in the deceased owner's gross estate for purposes of calculating the federal and state estate tax .
- If estate taxes are due at the death of the first partner, the estate might not have sufficient liquid assets to pay them.

- The asset is available to the owner's creditors during life (but not available to the survivor's creditors until the survivor receives the property in his or her own name at the death of the owner.)
- There is no mechanism to hold the asset in trust for the benefit of a disabled survivor.
- The survivor decides who gets the asset once it is transferred to the survivor's name regardless of what the original owner and the survivor had discussed prior to the original owner's death.
- They are not available in every state.

Contractual Property Rights

Many of us have contracts that entitle us to direct benefits to survivors at our deaths. Some of these contracts are associated with employee benefits at work. The most common examples of assets transferring via contract are insurance policies, retirement accounts, annuities and payable-on-death accounts.

Payable-on-death provisions to assets might appear to be the same as transfer-on-death deeds. They are not technically the same since they do not get their legal standing from state law but get it from internal policies offered by financial institutions. Therefore, they belong in the family of assets that transfer via contract provisions rather than by operation of law.

Trusts are technically part of this category, but will be discussed separately because of their unique features. They can be drafted to overcome many of the disadvantages of any other form of ownership and also provide disability planning.

The terms of the contract permit the owner to identify who receives the property under the contract when the owner dies. The owner must complete a beneficiary designation form identifying the beneficiary. The beneficiary designation form is the instruction sheet for the proceeds controlled by the contract.

A will has no power over the contract proceeds and will not direct who gets the benefits under the contract. The only exception to this rule is if the beneficiary form is defective for some reason or if the named beneficiary(s) dies before the owner dies and there is no one else named to take the benefit under the contract, or if the owner names their estate as the beneficiary. In this case, the contract will have an owner (who is deceased) but no named beneficiary. Therefore, probate will be needed to direct who gets the benefit.

We have seen disputes arise over failure to rename beneficiaries when people have entered into new relationships. Generally, the discovery is made that someone from a long ago relationship is still the named beneficiary on the retirement plan or insurance contract. The current partner is unhappy and inevitably brings a lawsuit to try and establish their rights. Our experience has been that most of the time the named beneficiary on the contract prevails.

Contract assets have some of the advantages of the other ownership methods discussed above

- There is no need for probate unless there is a problem with the beneficiary designation.
- There are no costs associated with creating the beneficiary designation.

- The transfer process is private and is not part of a court record.
- Some benefits are not considered income to the beneficiary so no income tax is due upon receipt.
- A trust can be named as a beneficiary to avoid issues associated with outright distributions.

Some disadvantages:
- The asset is available to the owner's creditors during life and may have been expended by the time of the owner's death.
- The asset can be included in the deceased owner's estate for purposes of calculating the federal and state taxable gross estate
- There is no mechanism for holding the asset for the survivor's benefit if the survivor is disabled at the time of the transfer
- The payout schedule for retirement benefits is less favorable for unmarried partners than it is for married partners. Generally, a spouse-beneficiary is afforded the opportunity to roll-over the account into his or her name and to continue the income tax deferral during the balance of their lifetime and potentially for the lifetime of their named beneficiaries. The ability to continue the income tax deferral is not available to non-spouses
- An unmarried owner can change the beneficiary any time prior to death or incapacity without the consent of the survivor; married couples cannot change the beneficiary from the spouse without the spouse's written consent.

A vivid example of how failure to plan and failure to update beneficiary forms can cause emotional and financial hardship for a family is the following case. An unmarried couple failed to properly designate each other on their life insurance beneficiary forms. They also failed to do any planning at all, and did not even have a will to protect each other. One partner died and at that time it was discovered that his father, not his partner, was the beneficiary on the life insurance policy. Sadly, the father was already dead. Therefore, the default language in the deceased partner's insurance contract provided that his estate—not his life alliance partner—was the beneficiary when a named beneficiary had already predeceased.

He did not have a will so the laws of intestacy controlled the disposition of the insurance proceeds. Under the rules of intestate succession his mother was the beneficiary of his entire estate. Unfortunately at the time, his mother was living in a nursing home, was receiving Medicaid and was mentally incapacitated. Her incapacity required the appointment of a guardian to handle the insurance proceeds. It was also necessary to implement a plan to protect her from becoming ineligible for Medicaid benefits due to the receipt of the insurance proceeds. That's the good news.

The bad news is the surviving girlfriend brought several lawsuits to establish her rights in their home (owned by the decedent), their vehicles (owned by the decedent), the life insurance (now paid to his estate) and his retirement plan. All of the litigation, the pain, the family trauma—all of it—could have been avoided had the couple taken the time to meet with an estate planning professional, prepare the proper estate planning directives and examine the ownership of assets and beneficiary designations affecting their assets.

Trusts

People can create trust to address their unique needs. They can have more than one type of trust, depending on their particular circumstances. Trusts can be what we call "living" trusts or "testamentary" trusts. They can be revocable or irrevocable. An explanation of these terms is below.

A trust only controls property that is held in the name of the trust. The process of changing the title of assets into the name of the trust is called "funding" or asset integration. Assets held in an individual's name or as joint tenants with rights of survivorship are not controlled by the trust terms.

Living trusts are in effect when they are signed—when we are living. These are also called *inter vivos* trusts, which is the Latin term meaning "between the living." The provisions in these trusts can include instructions and legal authority for taking care of the trustmaker and loved ones during the trustmaker's life, either while alive and well or in the event of disability, as well as the trustmaker's beneficiaries at the trustmaker's death.

Testamentary trusts are trusts that are created in someone's will. They do not exist until the maker of the will dies and the will is administered. Therefore, unlike living trusts, testamentary trusts must go through the probate process. Because a testamentary trust cannot come into existence until the maker of the will dies and the will that created the testamentary trusts is probated, a testamentary trust cannot provide instructions to take care of the maker or his or her loved ones during a period of disability in the maker's life.

Revocable trusts and testamentary trusts created in a will can be modified anytime up to the time the maker dies or becomes incompetent. In a revocable trust, the trustmaker can authorize others to modify the trust terms even when the trustmaker is incompetent or has died. The agent in the trust who is authorized to make changes is generally referred to as a "trust protector."

Irrevocable trusts are created during the trustmaker's life-time but they generally cannot be amended after creation, except by court order or under the direction of a trust protec-tor and with limitations.

There are many benefits of trusts:

- Trust terms are private since they do not require probate —a public process.
- They can include provisions for disability determination and explicit legal authority to take care of the trustmak-er and other loved ones even when the trustmaker is incompetent.
- Assets generally are not placed directly into the name of the beneficiary, thereby protecting the assets from being vulnerable to the beneficiary's creditors or to waste caused by the beneficiary.
- A trust can hold assets for a partner's use during the part-ner's lifetime, with the balance of the assets passing to others (perhaps children from a prior relationship) at the partner's death.

- Gift tax implications will not be triggered on the total sum as long as the asset is not placed into the name of the beneficiary.
- The interests of children from prior relationships or other family members will be protected because assets will not transfer outright to a survivor partner.
- Trust terms can be drafted to enhance the likelihood that payments from the trust supplement rather than supplant a beneficiary's needs-based public disability benefits, if any.
- If properly drafted, trusts can provide a way to manage assets while the survivor is coping with the grieving process.
- Unlike a will, the mechanisms for contesting a trust are more difficult than for wills.

Trusts have powerful possibilities for unmarried couples. Trusts permit unmarried couples to dodge and weave around many of the disadvantages of the other forms of disability and death planning options they may be most familiar with. Trusts can keep planning private and reduce the ability of hostile family members who might try to intervene.

Summary Regarding Ownership of Assets

The above mechanisms of transferring assets when an owner dies must be coordinated with the life alliance partners' legal directives to ensure that their goals are achieved. Married couples have the luxury of not having to pay particular attention to the sums they transfer to each other during life or at the death of the first spouse. Life alliance partners do not have this luxury because of the number of unintended consequences that may occur:

- Gift taxes
- Federal and state estate taxes
- Assets can lose the "step up in basis" for the purpose of calculating capital gains taxes when the asset is later sold
- Potential "due on sale" liability on mortgages.

Special Planning for Life Alliance Partners

Life alliance partners must undertake special legal and financial planning. The traditional vehicles used by married couples do not produce good results for them. Some additional areas to consider in the planning process are as follows:

- How should the plan deal with the unmarried survivor partner who does not work outside of the home and does not have comparable retirement funds as a result? Without proper planning, that partner could risk having inadequate retirement funds if he or she is not provided for by the other partner's benefits when the relationship ends by death or other means.
- Do the partners want to equalize their assets between them, and, if yes, how will this be accomplished with the least amount of gift tax consequences?
- How will the partners plan for different contingent beneficiaries? If the partners want to provide for the survivor during the survivor's lifetime and then other

beneficiaries when the survivor dies, how will the directives be prepared to ensure these other beneficiaries receive the first partner's property? Remember, once the asset is transferred to the survivor, the survivor can direct the asset to his or her own beneficiaries. There is no legal obligation for the survivor to direct the assets to the original partner's contingent beneficiaries after the survivor's death. An example of this problem might be a survivor who names a subsequent boyfriend or girlfriend as the beneficiary of an asset rather than the children of the first partner as they had agreed before the partner's death. Some partners, married and unmarried, have concerns about their assets being paid to later partners.

- How will estate taxes be paid if there is a federal and state taxable estate? Where will the money come from?

It should be clear that unmarried individuals have an obligation to themselves and to their partners to implement a comprehensive estate plan that addresses the needs of the individuals. Family members, children, pets and other loved ones can be provided for in a manner consistent with the wishes of the partners and not at the whim of the state in which the couple resides.

There are a number of potential solutions to the questions posed in this chapter. Some of the questions will be raised by your legal and financial advisors, and some must be raised by the you. This is particularly true if the advisors you work with do not have specific experience in dealing with the issues unique to life alliance partners. ♥

Chapter 6

Taxation and Gifts to Uncle Sam

*T*ax issues for unmarried couples and same-sex partners mimic those for single individuals, but the potential for unintended consequences is greater as their financial lives are entwined over time. Therefore, it is important to understand the rules as they apply to single taxpayers when making decisions about your tax life with your life alliance partner.

Income Taxes

Single taxpayers will pay taxes at the single taxpayer rate. This can have some advantages, especially if the U.S. government continues to penalize married taxpayers with the marriage penalty tax. The marriage penalty tax requires married couples to pay more tax on their combined income than a single person would pay on the same total income. For example, two single wage earners, each with an annual income of $50,000 per year, will each pay approximately $8,327 in income taxes. Together they pay a total of $16,654. If this same couple were to marry and file jointly, their tax liability will be approximately $18,172—a penalty of more than $1,500. However, in a few situations, getting married will result in lower taxes, such as when one partner doesn't work.

In some cases, unmarried partners can claim the other partner as a dependent on their income tax return—which qualifies them for an additional exemption and lower overall taxes. As for real estate capital gain taxes, unmarried partners selling their homes get the same tax shelter as do married couples.

However, if you live in a common law marriage state, common law marriage counts as a real marriage as far as income taxes are concerned. If you live in a state that recognizes common law marriage and you hold yourself out as married, you are married for federal tax purposes and should file accordingly. On the other hand, if a couple lives together with no intent to be married, they may file as single individuals even if they live in a state recognizing common law marriage. This is one instance where it may be important to create a written statement of your intent *not* to be considered married.

The marriage penalty is expected to be reduced, in part, by 2005. The 2001 Economic Growth and Tax Relief Reconciliation Act (EGTRRA) eliminates the marriage penalty tax for some couples. The marriage penalty tax is expected to be slowly phased out starting in 2005 and will be completely gone by the 2009. However, it only affects married couples who don't itemize deductions or who are in the 15% tax bracket. Couples who itemize their deductions or who are in a tax bracket higher than 15% will continue to pay a marriage penalty tax.

Dependents and Taxes

Taxpayers who live together may be able to claim one of the cohabitants as a dependent and qualify for an additional exemption if certain requirements are met. The IRS defines dependents as either close relatives or unrelated persons who live in the taxpayer's household as the principal place of abode and who are supported by the taxpayer.

Claiming Your Partner as a Dependent

Your life alliance partner may qualify as a dependent if they live with you;

- they are a U.S. citizen, a U.S. resident, or a resident of Canada or Mexico;
- they do not file a joint return with anyone else (for example, a spouse, if they are still married);
- they do not have $3,050 or more of gross (total) income in 2003; and
- they are supported —food, clothing, shelter, medical and dental care, education, and such (generally more than 50%) by you.

If you would like more information on claiming your life alliance partner as a dependent, consult your tax professional. You can also read IRS Publication 501, Exemptions, Standard Deductions and Filing Information. To get this publication, contact the IRS at 800-829-1040 or visit the IRS website at www.irs.gov.

Claiming Children as Dependents

Unmarried couples may also claim "head of household" filing status when they support a dependent other than the person they are living with. For example, if your child lives with you and your partner, you could file as head of household and get many of the same credits available to married filers, such as the earned income credit for wage earners with income below specific levels and child and dependent care credits. By filing as head of household, an unmarried taxpayer can claim both the child and the other adult to get dependency exemptions for a total of three (3) exemptions.

When parents are divorced or just live apart, the question of who gets to take the dependency exemption for federal income tax purposes often arises. Section 152 of the Internal Revenue Code provides that if the parents were once married, the parent who has physical custody for the greater part of the year and provides more than one half of the child's support gets to claim the exemption. You can change this by waiving your right to claim the exemption in a written agreement (for example, in a divorce, separation agreement or child custody agreement) or by filing a declaration with the IRS. You should consult your tax advisor to decide how to handle this situation. You can also read IRS Publication 504, Divorced or Separated Individuals, which you can download for free at www.irs.gov.

If you were never married, the test for determining the dependent exemption is simpler: whoever provides at least 50% of the child's supports gets the exemption.

Real Estate Taxes

Current tax law allows married couples to avoid taxes on the first $500,000 of capital gains (the interest and profit earned while owning a home) when they sell their home, as long as they've resided in the home for two out of the five years preceding the sale. Single individuals get a $250,000 capital gain tax exemption. Therefore, two unmarried individuals, each owning a half interest in a residence, could each qualify for the $250,000 exemption. This is one of the few areas of tax law where married couples and unmarried partners have the same result.

Social Security

Life alliance partners who live together are often at a disadvantage when it comes to Social Security benefits—especially if one partner stays at home caring for children or running the household.

Typically, you qualify for Social Security benefits based on your own earnings record. If you don't work at a job that pays Social Security tax, you don't earn credit towards Social Security benefits. But married couples get a benefit—spouses are eligible for certain Social Security benefits based on the other spouse's earnings record. These are called "dependent benefits" (which you get if your spouse qualifies for retirement or disability benefits) and "survivor benefits" (which you get if your deceased spouse or ex-spouse qualified for retirement or disability benefits). So, for example, if a husband stays at home and takes care of the kids for a number of years, he may still be able to collect Social Security benefits based on his wife's earnings record.

Couples who live together but are not married are not eligible for dependent or survivor benefits. This presents an obvious disadvantage when one partner in a life alliance arrangement works outside the home and the other works in the home, caring for kids or taking care of the household.

A stay-at-home partner could earn Social Security credits, however, if the other partner employed them to take care of the home and/or children. The "employer partner" would pay wages to the stay-at home partner and pay Social Security tax on the stay-at-home partner's behalf. Both partners would have to comply with other requirements as well. For example, the stay-at-home partner will have to pay state and federal income tax on the wages. And in many states, the "employer partner" will also have to pay disability insurance and other types of insurance or taxes.

Unmarried older couples may avoid taxes on their Social Security benefits by remaining unmarried. The marriage penalty is compounded by the fact that certain older married couples who have a modest income and receive Social Security benefits must pay tax on their benefits if their income is more than $32,000 annually. The IRS looks at the married couple's combined adjusted gross income, as reported on their tax return, plus interest from tax exempt investments plus 50% of their combined Social Security benefits. In contrast, each partner in an unmarried partnership pays taxes on Social Security benefits only if his or her income is more than $25,000. This means that, as an unmarried couple, their annual income could be as high as $50,000 before they have to pay taxes on Social Security benefits.

You should consult with your tax advisor or an attorney familiar with these benefits to determine how unmarried couples can benefit tax-wise when it comes to Social Security benefits. Or you may obtain information directly from the Social Security Administration.

Common Law Marriage

A common law marriage is just as valid as a formal marriage for purposes of receiving Social Security. This means if you live with someone covered by Social Security in a state that recognizes common law marriage and your partner has recently died or become disabled, you may be able to claim you were married under common law and, as a result, qualify for benefits.

Living with a life alliance partner, however, doesn't end Social Security benefits derived from a former marriage. If your spouse has died and you are receiving survivor's benefits or you are divorced, you can get benefits on your ex-spouse's Social Security account if your marriage lasted at least ten (10) years and you have been divorced two years (it makes no difference whether a former spouse has remarried or you are living with someone). Similarly, if you qualify for benefits as a divorced spouse and your former spouse has died, you can receive survivor's benefits as early as age sixty (fifty if you're disabled). You should consult with a tax or legal advisor who is familiar with these rules, contact a local office of the Social Security Administration or check their website at www.ssa.gov.

Public Benefits

People who receive public benefits often worry they will be cut off if their partner moves in. If you receive benefits based on your financial need and a physical or mental condition—aid to the aged, blind or disabled, for example—you don't risk any loss. Broadly speaking, these programs function like Social Security—once you qualify, you're largely left alone. When it comes to benefits based on financial need alone (and not on a physical condition), however, living with someone may affect your food stamp eligibility or the amount of aid you receive. This issue usually arises when a woman with children who is receiving welfare wants to live with her boyfriend or life alliance partner. The federal government delegates welfare rules to the states, which in turn, are experimenting with all sorts of policies. The best advice we can give you is to call an advisor experienced in these matters or your local social service department to make sure you understand the rules that affect you.

Depending on where you live, here is what you may find:

- Contributions towards household expenses—such as paying the rent or buying the food—made by someone you are living with will not affect the amount of your benefit.
- Cash contributions made by a life alliance partner may reduce the amount of your monthly benefit—but it can depend on how much is contributed and the purpose of the contribution.
- In a few states, a legal responsibility for all household members to contribute to the household is presumed. This means if you live with someone in these states, your welfare benefit will be reduced even if the person doesn't, in fact, assist with the monthly expenses.
- If you have registered as domestic partners, you may have signed a statement saying you will provide for one

another. This could, in theory, be used to deny one of you public benefits.

Gift Taxes

Under the current gift tax rules, annual gifts of up to $11,000 (current figure) per person per year are excluded from your lifetime gift tax limit—currently $1 million. This means you may give as many gifts of $11,000 or less each year to as many individuals as you desire without incurring a gift tax obligation or obligation to file a gift tax return. Married individuals, on the other hand, can give unlimited gifts to each other and may join together, called "gift-splitting," and give up to $22,000 per year to others for the purposes of making annual exclusion gifts.

Annual gifts can be a good way to transfer assets from someone who has assets in excess of the estate tax applicable exclusion amount (currently $1.5 million), or simply for the purpose of making lifetime gifts that can be enjoyed while the gift-giver is still alive and well.

If you loan your life alliance partner money, get a promissory note if it is important to you to be repaid. Otherwise, it may be considered a gift and depending on the size of the gift may impact your future ability to leave assets without an estate tax obligation. In addition, if the gift is more than $11,000 per year (called the annual gift tax exclusion amount) you may have also created an obligation to file a gift tax return (Form 709) and report the gift to the IRS.

A promissory note is the borrower's "promise to pay." It is the borrower's written acknowledgment that a debt exists. If a dispute over the debt arises, the lender would only have to prove to the court that the borrower failed to pay. The lender would be spared the expense of having to also prove that a debt existed and the amount of the debt.

Estate Taxes

An obligation to pay estate taxes depends on the size of your estate. Currently, if your estate at the time of death is less than $1,500,000 your estate will not be liable for any federal estate taxes. This can be a tricky area, however, because people are not always clear about what is included in their taxable estate.

Generally, we say that everything you own, everything you control and everything with your name on it gets counted for estate tax purposes. This means that all of your jointly held property gets included (at least a portion of it), everything you own individually, all your life insurance policies (not just the cash value but the death benefit value), your retirement plans including IRAs, 401ks, deferred compensation, and so forth—it all gets included.

The estate tax applicable exclusion amount—the amount we can leave estate tax free at our deaths—is currently scheduled to increase over the next few years until it is eliminated in the year 2010. However, it is scheduled to return to $1 million in 2011.

Without further government action, the estate tax applicable exclusion amount will be as follows:

2004—$1,500,000
2005—$1,500,000
2006—$2,000,000
2007—$2,000,000
2008—$2,000,000
2009—$3,500,000
2010—Unlimited—the estate tax is "repealed"
2011—$1,000,000—the estate tax returns

While married individuals can benefit from the unlimited marital deduction that allows one U.S. citizen spouse the ability to leave to another U.S. citizen spouse an unlimited amount of assets free from federal estate taxation, single individuals do not have this same benefit. Single people are limited to the "applicable exclusion amount," also called the "estate tax exemption amount," which is $1.5 million as of this writing. Therefore, in 2004 and 2005, a single person can leave up to $1.5 million to a partner completely free of estate tax. A married individual can leave an unlimited amount to his or her spouse without incurring any estate tax liability.

Estate taxes are essentially a voluntary tax in the sense that you can "volunteer" to pay them by failing to plan adequately. Avoiding the payment of unnecessary taxes requires education and planning. Seek out the advice of a qualified tax or legal professional to assist you in structuring your estate in a way that will minimize the estate tax effects on your estate.

Both income and estate tax planning require the assistance of legal and tax professionals. We don't recommend this area for do-it-yourselfers. There are too many ways to make costly mistakes.

The tax law changes are an example of why plans must be updated. Although legal and financial advisors create directives and build plans to withstand many of the anticipated changes in the law, partners' best interests are served if the plans can undergo scrutiny from time to time. In this way, the partners are less likely to be vulnerable to unanticipated dangers to their plans and are more likely to be able to take advantage of opportunities.

Chapter 11 discusses updating, education and maintenance in the context of planning for unmarried partners. ♥

Chapter 7

Life Alliance Agreements™

A contract is an agreement to do or not to do something. Marriage is a contractual relationship. Saying "I do" commits a couple to a well-established set of state laws and rules governing, among other things, the couple's property rights should one spouse die, become disabled or terminate the relationship.

Unmarried couples and same-sex partners don't have an automatic state-imposed contractual agreement when they begin a relationship. The couple may have a joint obligation to a landlord if they rent or to a mortgage company if they buy a home together, but under the law, their mutual obligations will be no different than if they were roommates.

Unlike marriage, living together as life alliance partners, in and of itself, does not create a legal contractual relationship. It does not entitle a one of the partners to a property settlement if the relationship ends or a partner becomes disabled and unable to work. It does not entitle one partner to the estate of the other partner when the partner dies. Even in the <u>Marvin</u> case the former girlfriend's right to property at the end of the relationship was based on more than her having cohabited with Mr. Marvin.

Unmarried couples buy property, mix assets, co-mingle finances and invest together. Their financial lives become entwined through their daily actions. More often than not, they fail to write down their intentions regarding ownership of assets. If problems about money and property arise, the couple can try to reach an understanding or compromise if there is a difference of opinion about their original intent, or they may find themselves in court.

Courts in most states have responded to such disputes by determining what the couple had verbally agreed to. The courts will then attempt to divide the couple's property accordingly. In doing so, courts have ruled that unmarried couples generally have the right to create whatever kind of life alliance agreement or contract they want when it comes to financial and property concerns.

A life alliance agreement—sometimes referred to as a "non-marital agreement"—is a contract between unmarried partners designed to specifically set out all the terms and conditions of the life alliance partnership. The agreement establishes the parties' intent regarding their rights to property both during lifetime and if the relationship ends. Under most circumstances, the agreement can be considered an enforceable contract.

Life alliance agreements are made to protect each partner in case the relationship ends and to provide clarity if there is some reason to present proof regarding the parties' intentions. More often, couples enter into these agreements to communicate their needs and expectations, define their rights and enhance one or both partners' peace of mind. The agreements may be made at any time during the relationship but are best advised in the beginning of a relationship or when the couple makes a major purchase. The important point to remember here is that it is better to have an agreement than to not have one.

Life alliance agreements are recommended to reduce current and future misunderstandings between partners. If the relationship never ends and the life alliance agreement is never needed, then the agreement is just good insurance against an unpredictable world. This is another "sweater in a suitcase." It is nice to have when you really need it.

Recall that before the Marvin case in the 1970s, couples who lived together without getting married existed in a legal vacuum. Prior to that case, the courts generally held that money and property belonged to the person who earned it or originally owned it. Contracts to share earnings or property usually weren't enforced by courts on the theory that the agreements were based on "meretricious consideration." Consideration is the price paid in a contract; meretricious means "resembling a prostitute." In effect, what the courts were saying was that contracts between unmarried individuals were illegal contracts for sex outside of marriage and an illegal contract cannot be enforced.

The Marvin court held that California divorce laws governing alimony and the division of property did not apply to unmarried couples. Instead, the court applied contract law principles rather than family law principles. However, without a contract of some kind, neither party will have any rights to the other's assets or for post-separation support. That is, unless the couple lives in a state that recognizes common law marriage and the couple meets the requirements for common law married status. For obvious reasons, this is not available to same-sex couples.

The general rule that marital property rules do not apply to unmarried couples has been widely adopted in other states. However, a few states that do not recognize common law marriage have nevertheless found ways to provide some property to a long-term life alliance partner when the relationship ends.

Today, following the reasoning of the <u>Marvin</u> case, the courts of nearly every state and the District of Columbia now recognize and enforce written contracts between unmarried couples and same-sex partners. Illinois, however, remains an exception to the general acceptance of contract rights for unmarried couples. The Illinois courts still hold that the "immoral" nature of living together prevents a couple from forming a contract and, consequently, a co-habitation agreement (or life alliance agreement) between unmarried partners will not be enforceable.[10] Further, the courts of some states have recognized that the legal concepts of "unjust enrichment" and "implied contract" can apply to disputes between unmarried couples.

The lesson to be learned here is that all unmarried couples, opposite and same-sex, should record all important elements of their relationship in writing—in the form of a contract or agreement, a life alliance agreement—and never rely on the courts to interpret their actions later. For unmarried couples who cannot or chose not to marry, a life alliance agreement is the alternative to the bundle of rights imposed by state law when a couple is married. You might not need an agreement if you have no assets or are in a brief relationship. But you should have one if you are in a long-term and serious relationship, or anytime you are contemplating common ownership of assets or investments, you should consider the legal consequences of co-mingling those assets and the effect common ownership might have if the relationship ends.

The Premarital Agreement Example

Premarital agreements were discussed in Chapter 3 as a way for people who plan to marry to modify the marriage contract that is imposed by state domestic relations laws. Premarital agreements allow you to establish your own property ownership rules and these rules can be significantly different from the state's marital property laws. A premarital agreement lets you agree in advance as to how much support one person will pay the other in case the relationship ends. Premarital agreements can offer an example for life alliance partners to follow when crafting their own agreements.

If you have a life alliance agreement and later get married, is the agreement still enforceable? The general rule is that if the agreement was created shortly before the marriage or at a time when both partners planned to be married, it is more likely to be enforceable since it has the qualities of a premarital or prenuptial contract. Premarital agreements must be made in contemplation of marriage.

Tips for Creating a Life Alliance Agreement:

1) Talk about what you want your agreement to include and reach an understanding on the major points. The partners should set some ground rules about how you will arrive at decisions and whether and when you will get outside help, such as an attorney, to guide you through the process. This can eliminate one potential source of tension by understanding how you will go about the process of reaching agreement.

Think about the before, during, and after phases of relationships and organize your decisions in these phases. The before phase is what the partners are bringing to the relationship. The during phase concerns how the partners plan to handle their day-to-day life together. This day-to-day phase can include the financial aspects as well as the more mundane aspects of who does the laundry and grocery shopping. The after phase concerns how the partners envision their rights to the property and income of the other partner, as well as their debts, when the relationship ends either due to death or some other reason.

The discussion that occurs during the creation of the agreement can be a good way for you to gain an understanding of the "living together" aspect of your relationship. At a minimum, this discussion can help clarify your mutual understanding of your expectations in the relationship. People are rarely disappointed if expectations are clearly defined early in a relationship.

2) List the assets, incomes and debts the partners are bringing to the relationship. Agree how you will define your rights to this property. Will you combine the property, income and debts immediately and share them equally? Will all property, income and debts remain separate? Will you share some property, income and debts and keep others separate?

Just as with premarital agreements, if the agreement is ever disputed in court, the court will be less likely to enforce an agreement that is based on trickery or an inherent unfairness, such as failure to disclose essential information. Therefore, you should follow the example offered by premarital agreements and fully disclose all material facts pertinent to the details upon which you are being asked to agree. Consider whether you should attach a list of the assets, income and debts you are bringing to the relationship. This will eliminate later confusion about whether a specific item was included in the original agreement. This will be an important aspect of your "paper trail" discussed in Chapter 10.

3) Come to an agreement regarding your financial affairs during the relationship. This involves a lot of considerations, such as: How will you handle income, property and debts acquired during the relationship? How will living expenses and responsibilities be shared—including income tax consequences (payments and deductions)? Who will be responsible for paying the bills and balancing the checkbook? Who will contribute what dollars to the financial requirements of the household? This may be especially important if one of you makes significantly more than the other or if one person had to make a major sacrifice in order to live with the other, such as moving a long distance or giving up a job to care for small children. Will a partner be reimbursed for contributions (money or services) contributed to the other partner's education? How will the finances be handled in the event of a long-term illness or mental incapacity?

4) How will the finances be handled if the relationship ends, either through death or otherwise? Will a partner receive compensation if the relationship ends and that

partner has forgone career opportunities to care for children and/or home, putting the at-home partner in a disadvantaged financial status? Do you intend to transfer property at the death of either partner, and if so, what property or categories of property will be transferred? Will there be a mechanism of priority or right of first refusal to permit the surviving partner to purchase assets from the deceased partner's estate? Who gets custody of the partner's pets?

What constitutes termination of the relationship (for purposes of the obligations under the agreement)? The rules governing married couples would call this "grounds" for a divorce.

5)   Don't try to cover everything in one agreement. Relationships and people are complicated. If you try to cover too many issues in one agreement, you may get bogged down and never complete your agreement. It might be better to have several smaller agreements covering specific issues. For example, your property agreement could be separate from whatever agreement you have to support a partner who's still in school. Your agreement on sharing housing costs and ownership could also be separate.

But be careful that separate agreements do not conflict, and be clear if you intend to undo a prior agreement with a later agreement.

6)   Don't get too personal. If your agreement includes personal as well as financial clauses, a court might declare the entire agreement illegal or frivolous and refuse to enforce

any of it—including the more important financial clauses. Obviously, you need to be clear with your partner on things such as house cleaning, childcare, pet care and bill paying. Just don't mix up these day-to-day issues with the bigger legal issues of sharing a life together.

7) Don't mention the intimate aspects of the relationship. This can cause the agreement to be found invalid if you end up in court. A life alliance agreement that is explicitly based on the performance of sexual services may be determined to be invalid by the courts in most, if not all, states. The courts are very sensitive to any implication that they are legitimizing any act of prostitution—hence the finding of "meretricious consideration." Even referring to one's partner as a "lover" has been held sufficient grounds to throw out a life alliance agreement.

8) Don't prepare a life alliance agreement for the purpose of sharing property if one or both of you are married to someone else. This is a legal area that has little clarity. If one of you is still married to someone else, your best course of action is to agree to keep everything separate until the marriage is officially dissolved and the marital property has been separated with the court's blessing. After the divorce is final, you can write a life alliance agreement and combine your property with your new partner if it is your intention to do so.

9) Get legal advice before signing any legal contract, especially a life alliance agreement. This is particularly true if one or both partners have a lot of money or property is involved or there are complicated estate planning issues

or if one partner has substantially more assets than the other. It is important to understand the laws as they apply in your state since they can vary considerably.

10) Get legal help if bargaining power or positions aren't equal. A life alliance agreement may not be enforceable if the court determines that one person has taken unfair advantage of the other. For example, a court is unlikely to uphold a one-sided agreement entered into between an experienced professional and an unsophisticated but wealthy nineteen year old who just moved to America and speaks little English, under which the inexperienced teen agrees to support the professional.

11) Get legal help if you live in Illinois. In Illinois, it's doubtful that any life alliance agreement is enforceable. Illinois courts remain opposed to the general acceptance of contract rights for unmarried couples. You may be able to create a life alliance agreement in Illinois by stating, in writing, that your agreement is simply a contract to share the ownership of certain property and has nothing to do with your personal relationship. Here, you may have to turn to business principles and solutions to address your property and financial concerns.

12) Each partner should have independent legal representation to avoid the inherent conflict of interest that would occur if one attorney tried to represent both parties. This is especially true if there is a significant difference in the financial standing or sophistication of the partners.

13) Agree in advance to mediate disputes that may arise over your agreement. Mediation is usually less expensive,

faster and less painful than litigation. Mediation is a process whereby a neutral third party assists the parties in reaching a decision without protracted litigation and without the ongoing expenses of litigation and attorney's fees. In mediation, parties can be creative to determine their own unique solutions. A mediator never decides a case, but helps facilitate negotiation and resolution.

If mediation fails, you can use arbitration as an alternate form of dispute resolution. In an arbitration process, one or more neutral arbitrators listen to the facts of the situation and then render a decision. Arbitration can be binding or non-binding. The parties agree before the process begins whether they will be bound by the arbitration panel's decision. Binding arbitration decisions are generally enforced in the same way that a judge's decision will be enforced. Some of the benefits of arbitration are that the time and costs involved can be more predictable and manageable. You can also agree to the division of attorney's fees and costs.

14) Don't attempt to agree on details that can't be honored by the courts. Parents are prohibited from making contracts regarding child support without court involvement. The domestic relations laws and courts of each state control child support matters. Generally, the rule is that a parent can't bargain away a child's rights and the law makes decisions for minors based on the best interests of the child.

15) The life alliance agreement doesn't need to be hard to read, full of legalese or anything that resembles what

you might be asked to sign if you were taking out a mortgage or buying a new car. A simple, comprehensive and functional document using common English is much better than one loaded with technical legal jargon. A contract doesn't have to sound technical or legal to be effective. You can, and should, design your life alliance agreement to say exactly what you both want, in words you both understand.

Many people find that creating a life alliance agreement forces them to deal with the core of their relationship. This is usually a healthy thing to do now and then—but it can also be trying. Take your time and don't expect to finish in an evening. A good life alliance agreement often involves compromise and accommodation. If you both feel you've given up a little more than you've received, you're probably on the right track.

Keeping Property Separate

Most unmarried couples keep all or most of their money and property separate—especially in the early years after they get together. The occasional exception might be a joint account to pay household bills or an agreement to jointly purchase one or more items of personal property.

You may think that keeping your property ownership separate is so simple that you don't need a written agreement. However, remember the many layers of laws and legal principles that can be brought to bear on your relationship regardless of your intent. Most states recognize oral contracts between unmarried couples. The lack of a written agreement can be an invitation for one partner to later claim the existence of an oral agreement to share property. This is what commonly occurs in "palimony" cases.

To avoid the possibility of future misunderstandings concerning property ownership, an agreement to keep property separate will memorialize your agreement. This agreement should identify all of the property you intend to keep separate, including property you brought into the relationship as well as property you purchased or received by gift or inheritance while living together.

Agreements for Sharing Property

If you currently own jointly purchased property or are considering a joint purchase, you may treat property that either of you purchases as jointly owned. If this is your intent, identify this specific property in the agreement.

Agreements for Special Types of Property

Creative people often work on inventions, software programs, artwork or books that are created over a period of time. It is often unclear how much monetary value, if any, the finished product will have. If you keep all your property and income separate, and have a written agreement to this effect, valuing these creative projects should not be a problem. Each partner will own what he or she has created.

However, if you agree to co-mingle the property you accumulate as a couple, you could run into problems valuing your creation if you split up. Suppose for example that you are a successful writer who's been working on a writing project for a couple of years. If you split up, who knows whether this yet-to-be-published book will sell five thousand copies, a million copies or some number in between? Even if you happily agree to divide your property when you separate, you may have real difficulty doing it fairly if there are unknown monetary considerations that have yet to be realized.

One solution is to keep your property separate. This can be accomplished with a separate property agreement. However, if you are determined to own everything jointly, including creative projects generated by one or both parties, your life alliance agreement will need a system for valuing unsold works and works in progress at separation. If you are both creators, one alternative is to simply say that, at the end of the relationship, "what's yours is yours and what's mine is mine." Another possibility is to set a date after separation at which time all creative work will be sold and the proceeds divided according to some formula. Works that aren't sold in this time frame (such as two or three years) could be owned outright by their creator. If the creative work in question is likely to be valuable, have a lawyer review your life alliance agreement before signing on the dotted line.

The selection of a competent valuation professional may also pose a problem. This issue may also be addressed in your agreement. You could agree on the method for selecting a valuation expert or, in the event of disagreement, each partner could select their own expert and the resulting values can be averaged.

Agreements for Business Owners

Business owners face many of the problems discussed above regarding creative individuals. If one partner starts a business during the course of the relationship and the business becomes successful, and later the relationship ends, thereafter it is important to know, in advance, how this property will be shared. This is especially important if one partner doesn't technically have an ownership interest but finds himself contributing significant amounts of time, talent and energy to the success of the business.

All business owners should have a buy-sell agreement or other written agreement that details how the business will be valued and divided if one of the business partners either wants out of the business for personal reasons (such as retirement), becomes disabled or dies. Inevitably, there is an expectation that the business has significant value. Determining in advance how this value will be calculated can help prevent litigation and unhappy outcomes later on.

The purchase of a life insurance policy may be one solution to raising the capital necessary to supply the consideration required in the buy-sell agreement.

An Unmarried 'Divorce'

Nothing lasts forever—or so they say. Like marriage, unmarried relationships can also end. Unlike marriage, the dissolution of an unmarried relationship may not be as complicated as a divorce—but don't count on it. As long as you and your partner can agree about how the property will be divided when you split, there might not be any reason to get lawyers and a court of law involved. However, if you can't agree or if you haven't taken steps to ensure your legal rights, your separation can be a legal nightmare. The best time to make these plans is now—when everything is going great and there are no bitter emotions to cloud the issues.

Each state's rules will be different, but the basic legal principles that govern the property rights of unmarried couples can be summarized as follows:

- Laws governing married couples and divorce do not apply—unless you live in a state that recognizes common law marriage and your relationship qualifies for that status. If you have a common law marriage, you will be required to follow the rules for divorce just as if you had formally married.

- Each unmarried partner is presumed under the law to own his or her own property and/or debts. This is true unless you have a deliberately combined your assets (such as acquiring property jointly in both names). This is different from married couples, where any debt or asset acquired by either spouse during the course of the marriage is usually considered a marital asset or debt in the event of a divorce. This is true unless the married parties signed a valid prenuptial agreement modifying these rules.

- The legal presumption of separate and independent property ownership by unmarried partners can be overcome by a written life alliance agreement designed to demonstrate it was the couple's intention to share assets and obligations. In some states, oral or implied agreements to share assets can be enforced. It is important to keep good records regarding contribution to assets. These records may be necessary to rebut a presumption that 100% of the value of an asset is included in the estate of the first to die.

The dissolution of a non-marital relationship may be governed by the same rules as the dissolution or winding up of a business, rather than a marriage. This might mean, unless you have an agreement to the contrary, that you won't have any of the advantages of mediation or arbitration. The exception will be if you have child-custody or child-support issues to resolve. In that case, the state laws regarding domestic relations will control and the family law division of your local court would hear the matter. The court will generally not become involved in matters outside of the custody and child-support issues.

Generally, unmarried couples are not entitled to any form of alimony or palimony for ongoing support after a breakup unless there is proof of a clear agreement to provide post-separation support. In some states, this will require a written agreement. Evidence indicating that one partner supported the other during the course of the relationship or even the presence of wills or trusts that indicate a desire to provide for a partner in the event of death may not be sufficient evidence. Married couples, on the other hand, are generally entitled to spousal support if one party has been financially dependent on the other, or if one person earned significantly more than the other.

The end of a relationship is never pretty. Protect yourself by clearly understanding the rules that affect your relationship in the event it ends. Carefully consider the acquisition of assets with your life alliance partner and what your ongoing financial relationship will look like. When in doubt, consider a life alliance agreement or other form of agreement to spell out the financial terms of your relationship. Then, if the worst happens, you are more likely to have some protections. ♥

Chapter 8

Solutions for Life Alliance Partners — A Matter of Trust?

The prior chapters discuss the areas where life alliance partners are vulnerable to problems during health, during disability and at death. We covered the options that married couples have and why many of these options won't work for unmarried couples. These discussions might lead you to believe unmarried couples don't have many options to protect themselves. But the answer is, they can use a number of the same tools married couples often use for a full range of planning objectives—for example, revocable living trusts, irrevocable life insurance trusts, special annuity trusts and family foundations. Unmarried couples can also use some concepts from business such as limited liability partnerships, limited liability corporations and buy-sell agreements. In addition, they can augment their plan with insurance to be certain that their partner has the financial wherewithal to survive when the first partner passes away.

Trusts

As briefly discussed in the chapters on disability and death planning, trusts can include instructions for managing assets when both partners are alive and well, during a period of disability for one or both of the partners, and when one or both of them pass away. A trust can incorporate the terms the couple created in a life alliance agreement(s) and can even be a substitute for some of the functions of a life alliance agreement. In fact, a trust can incorporate almost every element of the relationship between the couple, as well as their individual relationships with children from prior relationships or their obligations to other family members. If the trust is properly funded, the trust instructions can become a very effective and powerful tool to protect the interests of both partners and their other loved ones—even when they intend to ultimately benefit children from prior relationships.

Some advantages of using a revocable living trust as one of the core estate planning directives for unmarried couples are as follows:

- It is effective during the trustmaker's lifetime. This means it is already in place to handle daily interactions and the relationship to the partners' combined assets.

- Effectiveness during lifetime also means that it is in place to take care of the trustmaker during any periods of mental incapacity. There is no delay or cost associated with collecting proof to go to court to have a declaration of incapacity made by the court. There are no court costs associated with annual reports to the court regarding the ward's assets thereafter.

- The trust maintains the privacy of the trustmaker during lifetime, during disability and at death because there is no need, except under rare circumstances, to resort to the courts to get authority to act for the trustmaker. This assumes, of course, that the trust properly controls the trustmaker's assets.

- The priority of those who are authorized to act for the trustmaker during disability and at death is controlled by the trustmaker, who creates the terms of the trust.
- In addition to privacy, the mechanism to administer the trust during disability and at death is generally easier than a living probate (guardianship) or death probate.
- The trustmaker can amend the trust or even revoke it prior to mental incapacity or death. The trustmaker can include provisions for a "trust protector," which will allow the trust protector to make modifications to the trust if they are in the best interests of the beneficiary and consistent with the stated goals of the trust.
- The trust clauses can be drafted in such a way to protect the assets from the creditors of a surviving partner or to maintain and augment the survivor/beneficiary's entitlement to needs-based public assistance benefits.
- The trust clauses can be drafted to make the assets available to the surviving partner without having them included in the deceased partner's gross taxable estate. Conversely, the trust can be drafted to keep the deceased partner's assets out of the surviving partner's estate.
- Assets in the trust can be held for the benefit and use of the surviving partner during his or her lifetime but then pass to the first-to-die partner's family members at the death of the second partner. This is a solution to the "he who dies last controls the asset" problem which can trouble couples with children from prior relationships.
- Holding assets in trust for the surviving partner can make them less vulnerable to exploitation by later partners.

- Life alliance partners can construct the trust instructions to help avoid or to minimize the obligation to pay estate taxes.

- If the life alliance partners own property in another state titled in the name of the trust, they will not need a probate, called an ancillary probate, in the other state. This can save them time, expense and inconvenience.

The major disadvantages of trusts as a solution for life alliance partners might be thought to be the costs associated with having them prepared. If you equate the cost of having a trust drafted as its only value, a trust might appear to be more costly than a will, for instance. However, if you look at the higher level of protection that trusts can give you and your loved ones during life, during disability and at death, trusts are very cost effective.

The other disadvantage of trusts only applies if you fail to have your assets properly titled into the name of the trust. This is not an inherent disadvantage of a trust, but is a curable disadvantage.

Depending on how complicated your situation is, you can even create a variety of trusts to accomplish a variety of goals. Therefore, you could have a revocable living trust and an irrevocable life insurance trust, and you could name different beneficiaries for the various trusts. This may seem a little overwhelming at first, but if you focus on the objectives you want to achieve, trusts usually offer some of the best solutions—*if* they are well drafted and funded.

Disability Panel and Disability Trustee

Chapter 4 discussed the legal mechanisms of deciding when someone is mentally incapacitated. We discussed the use of a disability panel to make the declaration of the trustmaker's mental incapacity. We discussed the use of a disability trustee to manage the trust assets for the benefit of the disabled trustmaker and anyone else the trustmaker identified in the trust document.

The trust document can contain all of the instructions required for taking care of the disabled trustmaker and his or her loved ones, including children from prior relationships and even pets.

Death Trustee

The Chapter 5 discussion about how matters are handled when we die pointed out some situations where life alliance partners are at a disadvantage in terms of their standing in the eyes of the law and their ability to give assets to each other without triggering taxes or losing control. A trust can help them mimic many of the advantages married couples enjoy regarding tax advantages and creating protections for the ongoing control and management of assets for loved ones.

One of the advantages that married couples enjoy is the unlimited gifts they can pass to each other during life and at death. Even married couples, however, must plan for what happens to their assets at the death of the second spouse if they are concerned about paying unnecessary estate taxes. They commonly address this concern by using trusts called by a variety of names: A-B trusts, credit shelter trust, coupon trust, or a trust with marital and family sub-trusts. The terms mean that the trust was drafted in such a way that the assets in the trust are divided into two sub-trusts at the death of the first spouse. The first sub-trust is called the marital or the A trust. The second sub-trust is called the family or B trust.

The basic premise is that the assets are held in the name of the trust or sub-trusts for the benefit of the survivor at the death of the first (spouse or partner). When the survivor dies, the amount held in the trust or sub-trust is either distributed outright to the beneficiaries named by the original trustmaker or remains held in trust for their benefit during life.

The amount of the assets sub-trusts hold can be calculated by a variety of formulas. The legal community normally has an ongoing debate about which formula is the best for ensuring that maximum use of the applicable exclusion amount is obtained. What this means is that every individual can give a total of a specific dollar amount to others at death. The current figure for 2004-2005 is $1.5 million dollars. This exclusion amount is sometimes referred to as a "coupon" because it is like having a coupon that is good for a specified amount off of your gross estate before federal estate taxes apply.

Married couples each have a coupon for $1.5 million, which gives them a total of $3 million they can transfer at death if they use their coupons effectively. They are not penalized, as life alliance partners would be, if they transfer all or part of their coupon amounts to each other during life or at death. Therefore, married couples have a lot more flexibility when deciding how and when to use their coupons.

The standard instructions incorporated in most trusts for married couples is to have their trusts divide the deceased spouse's trust assets into a marital or "A trust" sub-trust and a family or "B trust" sub-trust. The marital sub-trust is for the benefit of the surviving spouse, and the spouse has access to principal and income from that trust according to the instructions set forth by the trustmaker when the original trust was created.

The family sub-trust is for the benefit of the spouse and children of the couple or, perhaps, some other beneficiaries. The trustmaker can state whether the surviving spouse has full, limited or no access to the principal and income of the family trust. The instructions will also specify the conditions under which the children or other beneficiaries of the family trust will have access to its assets and income.

For unmarried partners, the trust instructions can include provisions for dividing the assets into sub-trusts that keep the total assets below the level where federal estate taxes will apply. Or, the trust can help the partners avoid the issues associated with "he who dies last controls" JTROS property by including instructions to provide for the survivor partner *and* provide for other beneficiaries at the same time or when the second partner dies.

The beneficiaries do not need to be the same for each partner. This mechanism can help life alliance partners avoid the problem described in Chapter 5 regarding the married couple with children from prior marriages. In that situation the children from the deceased spouse's prior marriage were basically disinherited because all of the assets owned by their father transferred outright to his second spouse. The survivor spouse did not give any of her husband's assets to his children from that prior marriage, as was his desire.

Life alliance partners can take care of the survivor partner and then take care of others without losing control as they would with assets distributed outright via a will or via JTROS or contract beneficiary forms. They can structure their trust to be similar to a marital credit shelter trust. Instead of naming the survivor's share a "marital" trust, they might call it a "partner's" trust. They can also create a family trust like a married couple if they have other beneficiaries they want to take care of. Alternatively, they can just have their assets held for the benefit of the survivor in the partner trust with instructions to pass anything left in the trust to others when the partner dies.

Trusts permit life alliance partners to take care of themselves during lifetime, during disability and at death. They can avoid federal estate taxes the way married couples do by splitting the assets into sub-trusts. They do not lose control over the assets, however, because the trust instructions they create will remain in place and control the final disposition of assets and their use after both partners have died.

Life alliance partners can create a gift schedule to permit them to contribute assets to the trust in such a way that they will not exceed the annual amount a person can give others before triggering gift taxes. This schedule should be worked out with a legal and tax planning specialist or financial planner.

In essence, the trust can be drafted in such a way that it is a self-contained mechanism to handle every aspect of a person's life.

Additional Strategies

Trust Alphabet Soup

Estate planners always seem to be coming up with new ways to create trusts to meet the challenges of income, gift and estate tax laws. These trusts can be separate from, and can augment the instructions in, the core revocable living trust. These trust strategies are generally referred to by their acronyms, such as GRATs, ILITs and the like.

The initials in the acronyms reflect the prominent feature of the trust. For instance, a GRAT refers to a "grantor retained annuity trust," and an ILIT refers to an "irrevocable life insurance trust." The basic concept behind most of these strategies is that ownership is held in such a way that it is not included in your gross estate for purposes of calculating estate taxes, or the value that is included is substantially discounted in relation to the value received by the beneficiaries.

A detailed discussion of the features or merits of these strategies is beyond the scope of this book. Suffice it to say that these strategies can achieve a number of objectives to take care of the competing needs of the survivor partner and other beneficiaries, if need be, while avoiding unnecessary estate taxes.

One of these tools, however, requires a little discussion. It is one of the most familiar of the advanced planning tools. The tool is an irrevocable life insurance trust or ILIT. This is particularly useful for life alliance partners who have significant wealth; for when there is a significant disparity of wealth between the partners; or for when one is a homemaker while the other is the breadwinner, contributing unequal income to the relationship. The basic premise of an ILIT is that it permits the partners to overcome the disadvantages inherent in owning life insurance outright.

The basic rules regarding life insurance are that the death proceeds, not just the cash value, will be included in the owner's federal gross estate for purposes of calculating federal estate taxes unless the policy is given away. If the policy is given to another person or entity, such as a trust, it is no longer considered owned by the individual and, therefore, is no longer included in the owner's gross taxable estate. One exception to this rule would be if the owner retained "incidents of ownership." Incidents of ownership are not defined by the IRS, but examples can be found in IRS regulations. Basically, an incident of ownership makes reference to the right of the insured or his estate to the economic benefits of the policy. Therefore, an incident of ownership includes the power to change the beneficiary, to surrender or cancel the policy, to assign the policy, to revoke an assignment, to pledge the policy for a loan, or to obtain from the insurer a loan against the surrender value of the policy. In one case, a couple died in a plane crash where they had purchased their plane tickets with their platinum American Express card that provided a $500,000 death benefit. This death benefit was included in the deceased's gross estate for estate tax purposes. The deceased had the right to change the beneficiary pursuant to the terms of the credit card agreement, and that incident of ownership was sufficient to include the life insurance proceeds in their taxable estate.

One exception to the rule for removing life insurance from your estate upon transfer is when the insured/owner of the policy fails to survive for three years after the transfer. This is to prevent people from making transfers of life insurance on their death-bed in an attempt to remove the death benefit value from their taxable estate. Where an insured retains either incidents of ownership or dies during the three years following the transfer of the policy, the IRS will find that the policy is included in the gross taxable estate of the insured.

A properly drafted and funded ILIT permits the trustmaker to accomplish the following:

- avoid federal estate taxes on the value of the insurance proceeds at the death of one or both life alliance partners;
- control the insurance proceeds via the trust for the benefit of the people named in the trust; and/or
- create sufficient wealth and liquidity for the beneficiaries to cover expenses or pay estate taxes that might be due or to replace the income lost when the first partner died.

There are many other advantages that an ILIT can offer life alliance partners. It is considered an advanced estate planning technique. Partners considering an ILIT should include a financial planner or tax advisor on their planning team to determine the optimum amount of insurance required for their purposes as well as the schedule of premium payments and amounts to avoid inadvertently triggering gift taxes. These and the other technical requirements of ILITs should not dissuade life alliance partners from looking into how they might use them to their advantage.

Life Estates

A life estate gives someone the right to use an asset during their life. The ownership of the asset is transferred to someone else subject to the life tenant's right to use the asset during life.

In the context of planning for life alliance partners, a life estate could be used where a partner with children from a prior relationship transfers ownership of their house to the children subject to the life estate of the surviving life alliance partner. At the death of the second partner, the children will have full ownership of the property. Two objectives will be achieved— the survivor partner will have a home during life and the children's inheritance in the home would be protected for their future benefit.

Life estates are very familiar tools for most estate planning attorneys. The attorneys should counsel the partners on some of the disadvantages of life estates which include:

- The surviving partner might not be able to maintain the house if they do not have sufficient assets to support maintenance and repairs.
- The survivor might face mental incapacity or other disability which might make remaining in the home impossible.
- The homestead protection laws of the state where the property is located may not provide creditor protection when the home is left to a "non-heir."
- The property may be less marketable while the life estate exists because few people will be willing to buy property that carries the contingency associated with a life estate (unless all parties agree).

- If the life tenant fails to maintain the property, the ultimate beneficiaries might receive a damaged asset and might have limited or no legal recourse to seek reimbursement.

The deed to the property can include language to address some of these concerns, but life estates can be problematic, particularly if the competing interests of a life alliance partner and children from prior relationships have the potential for litigation. Either party to the deed would have to seek remedies from the court system, a process that can be both slow and costly.

Family Foundations

Family foundations are charitable planning solutions for individuals that want to minimize their federal estate tax exposure. A family foundation can be created for the purpose of providing the surviving partner and/or other family members with meaningful employment while at the same time accomplishing philanthropic objectives.

Strategies from Business

The business world has some tools that can be used by life alliance partners to address some of their needs. Business solutions to the issues concerning life alliance partners will treat the partners as business partners in the eyes of the law. The business partners will be required to comply with all of the filing, reporting and other requirements any business entity is required to follow. The trade-off is that the partners will have a set of well-established rules to guide them through their transactions and even through the termination of the relationship.

Courts have statutory and case law to guide them regarding the relationship between the partners. The court will only be able to address the business relationship (not the personal relationship), but at least it will have jurisdiction and prior law as the yardstick to follow.

The business tools and strategies can offer some other mechanisms to hold title and to value assets. This discussion will not be exhaustive but is offered to illustrate how planners guiding life alliance partners can "think outside the box" when considering solutions for their clients' unique needs.

Limited Liability Partnerships (LLPs) and Limited Liability Companies (LLCs). LLPs and LLCs offer an alternative to JTROS categories of property ownership. An LLP or LLC is formed with a partner who donates property to the entity and the other partner receives a non-controlling interest in the LLP or LLC. The entity's operating agreement outlines the obligations and rights of the partners and should have provisions for a buyout if the relationship should end.

This arrangement still raises gifting and gift tax considerations since the partner who did not contribute an equal amount to the entity will have received a gift in the eyes of the IRS. However, the partners may be able to take the position that the business value the lesser contributing partner received is discounted due to his or her lack of control in the entity as well as the reduced marketability of the entity interest.

LLP and LLC arrangements can also offer a higher level of creditor protection for the partners than other forms of ownership, such as JTROS. The creditors of the partner with the non-controlling interest will be limited to the actual distributions made from the entity to that partner, rather than having access to the entire property in the name of the entity. The creditor will also have income tax consequences for distributions, either realized or unrealized, that can reduce the net sums collected by the creditor. These factors may make collection attempts less attractive for the partners' creditors.

Buy-Sell Agreements. In the context of the business world, buy-sell agreements are the equivalent of premarital agreements. The agreement sets forth the terms and conditions regarding termination of the business relationship or, in this case, the life alliance partnership. Termination can be due to retirement, disability, death or other reasons.

Generally, the buy-sell agreement involves the use of insurance policies, either disability insurance or life insurance, to compensate the non-departing partner for the economic loss caused by the departure of one of the partners due to disability or death. Similar provisions can be incorporated into the life alliance agreement between partners. There are several ways insurance can be structured to enhance the likelihood that the insurance will properly compensate the partners when one of them becomes disabled or dies.

Obviously, business solutions for life alliances require input from financial advisors to determine the proper amounts of insurance required; valuation experts to properly value the assets and underlying business interests; certified public accountants to insure that all IRS and tax requirements are met; and from estate planning attorneys to assist in the drafting of any legal documents. The advisors should work as a team with frequent and open communication in order to meet the specific objectives of the partners.

Other Strategies

Some other matters life alliance partners might want to consider are set forth below. Again, this is not an exhaustive list but is representative of some of the more common issues presented when planning for committed, unmarried partners.

Name Changes

Name changes can be used by unrelated parties to convey a sense of relatedness and to reduce confusion or awkwardness that some people feel when explaining why a couple has a different last name. Obviously, the name change alone will not bring with it the automatic rights and privileges of being married or next of kin. Unmarried couples may use one partner's name or they may elect to use a hyphenated combination of both partners' names.

The rules governing changes of name are specific to each state. Most state laws will permit name changes for any reason as long as there is not an illegal purpose for the change, such as defrauding creditors.

The party who desires a name change must normally petition the probate court where they live and follow the specific court rules for such procedures. The court will usually publish a notice in a daily newspaper of the impending name change. If no objections to the change are raised, the court will issue an order changing the name and, thereafter, the party's legal name will be the one approved by the court.

Some people bypass the legal method for changing their name and simply begin using a new name. This is an accepted method of changing your name, but may result in unwanted issues with government authorities, such as the driver's license office, Social Security office or passport authorities.

On a practical note, even though a person's name change may have been ordered by a court, it is not uncommon for financial reporting agencies and other entities such as schools or employers to continue to list the person's former name along with the new name with connectors such as "also known as" or "formerly known as" or even "nee." Thereafter, whenever the person's name is listed, there is a list of names trailing the new one. This can defeat some of the motivation the person had to formally change his or her name, so we recommend that anyone contemplating this action consult with an attorney to discuss the pros and cons.

Parenting Agreements

A parenting agreement is a written agreement between the legally recognized parent (biological or adoptive) and the parent's partner who is to be considered the child's co-parent. There cannot be more than one legally recognized parent for a parenting agreement to apply.

The agreement documents the co-parents' mutual intent regarding their relationship, responsibilities, decision-making and rights regarding the child(ren). It establishes that the family exists, how the partners intend to deal with custody and visitation if the co-parents' relationship ends, or how they will resolve these issues, such as through mediation, if they can't agree.

There is no full faith and credit provisions where such relationships are considered against public policy. Therefore, in states like Ohio that have passed legislation to prohibit same-sex marriages, co-parenting agreements between same-sex partners might not be enforceable on the theory that it is against Ohio's public policy even if the agreement was considered valid in the originating state.

Guardianship

Biological parents retain certain rights in relation to their children even if they are not married—unless, of course, they have done something to forfeit those rights. Their unmarried status alone is not a barrier to those rights. Therefore, in the context of guardianships of minor children, the biological parents have priority over non-biological partners or relatives unless it is not in the best interests of the child to grant guardianship in the parent.

Unmarried couples, where one of the partners is the biological parent, must take specific steps to increase the likelihood that the non-biological partner is named guardian in the event something happens to the biological parent while the child is a minor. This is true in the case of all life alliance partners.

The biological parent-partner could create a will and nominate the non-biological partner as guardian in the event that the biological parent dies while of any the children are minors. The courts will not be required to adopt the nomination, but will generally give it consideration. Each state has its own set of guardianship laws.

As part of a comprehensive estate plan that involves minor children, you should consider a durable power of attorney for childcare that appoints the life alliance partner as agent for healthcare decisions for the minor child if the biological parent is unavailable. Most states have no statutory authority for such a power of attorney, but written authorization from the biological parent can be valuable protection for the minor child in the event of an emergency.

Adult Adoption

Adult adoption is sometimes offered as a mechanism of creating a legal relationship between partners. Under adult adoption procedures, one partner adopts the other. The adoptee becomes the adopting partner's "heir at law." Obviously, this strategy does not create a partnership status similar to that of marriage but it will invoke legal "relatedness" between the partners. There may be instances where this strategy is desired to create the heir at law status between the partners.

Adult adoption procedures are controlled by state laws. Some states do not permit adult adoptions, or they limit them to situations where the person being adopted, called the adoptee, is permanently disabled or is mentally impaired or where the parties had a step, or foster-parent relationship prior to the adoptee reaching the age of majority. Therefore, it is important to understand the requirements and procedures for the state in which you will be seeking an adult adoption.

The probate court will rule on the petition for adoption and determine whether the adoption is in the best interests of the adoptee. There are appeal processes if the decision is not favorable.

The adoptee does not have to adopt the name of the adopting partner, but could if the parties choose to do so. Once the adoption is approved, it cannot be undone if the parties no longer wish to be related. In addition, the adopted party gives up all inheritance rights by intestacy to his or her biological parents.

Property Loss

Partners should include each other as a named insured on the other's casualty insurance to enhance the likelihood that they will be adequately compensated in the event of a property loss caused by an insurable event. Otherwise, they might bear the economic costs associated with replacing lost property.

Summary

Attorneys who are experienced in planning for life alliance partners have an arsenal of planning tools to address their unique needs. Some of these strategies are based on long-standing legal principles and some are based on new laws. Either way, legal professionals who do not regularly plan for life alliance partners will be less likely to draw upon the full arsenal of tools that can be used, and may be guilty of making incorrect assumptions regarding factors entering into the decision-making process. ♥

Chapter 9

Fiduciaries, Attorneys and Other Scary People

*P*reparing and implementing your estate plan is not an endeavor you should do yourself. You should only work with knowledgeable professionals who have an expertise in estate planning and have knowledge specifically in the area of working with unmarried couples and same-sex partners. Legal specialization is becoming the norm. Family law attorneys specialize in divorce, child custody and other family law matters. Medical malpractice attorneys work in the area of seeking redress for injuries caused by medical personnel. If you are buying a home, you utilize the services of a real estate attorney. Effective estate planning requires a high degree of specialized knowledge and expertise. Generalists, or "threshold attorneys," (those who take any case that can cross the threshold), do not possess the knowledge or expertise necessary to provide comprehensive planning services or the ability to keep pace with future law changes—particularly in the area of planning for life alliance partners.

If you have minor children, identifying and selecting a future guardian, conservator or trustee for your child is required. The choice of guardian, conservator or trustee is critical to the future care and well-being of your child, especially after both parents or life alliance partners are gone. In addition to selecting who will raise your child consistent with your values and beliefs, families need to give careful thought as to who will manage money on the child's behalf. The laws pertaining to guardianship, conservatorship and trustees generally vary from state to state. It is important that your choice of trustee—the individual who will be responsible for managing the assets and making distributions be very knowledgeable, skilled and extremely diligent.

These are some of the issues you should consider:

- Who will manage the trust assets? The manager of a trust is called a "trustee." A trustee can be any person over eighteen years of age, a bank trust company, a financial planner, a CPA or other professional fiduciary. The trustee holds, administers and distributes all property allocated to the trust for the benefit of the trust beneficiaries during their lifetime.

- What skills or qualifications should this person have? The person you select as trustee should be someone who has an aptitude for investments, is detail oriented and will take the responsibilities of managing your money for the benefit of your children or other beneficiaries very seriously. He or she also needs to be someone who has high attention to detail and enjoys keeping books and records.

Trusts are not only necessary for minor children but also serve a very important function in revocable living trust planning. A trustee may serve as a disability trustee, a death trustee during administration or as a trustee for a lifetime trust for the benefit of your life alliance partner or other beneficiaries.

More Thoughts on Trustees

It is one thing to leave resources to a trust, and quite another to manage them in such a way as to last for the benefit period stated in your trust for your beneficiaries. Every trust must have a trustee, someone who will manage the trust's assets. In the case of a small trust—a trust whose assets are less than $500,000—a corporate trustee may not be willing to provide trust services. In some cases, the costs may outweigh the benefits. Unfortunately, few banks are willing to manage cash assets under several hundred thousand dollars or become as involved in your beneficiary's life as you would wish. Your choices are varied—you can select an individual, or several individuals to act as successor trustees, or you can select a bank trust department or a trust organization. A corporate trustee is always a good trustee of last resort, even if you wish to name individuals or family members as your initial successor trustees. You never know when an individual or family member will be unable or unwilling to serve in the role of successor trustee.

Sensitizing Fiduciaries

Guardians and trustees are commonly referred to as "fiduciaries." Fiduciaries are appointed in a will or in a trust to assume the responsibilities of decision-making in the absence of the primary decision-maker. The manner in which these duties are exercised is of paramount concern to the person making the appointment. It is not enough to simply leave the duty or responsibility to a person in whom you have faith or trust, a foundation for decision-making must be established. By doing so you help to ensure preservation of family values and to resolve issues that may otherwise create uncertainty in the mind of the appointed fiduciary.

Instructions within the estate plan documents should establish a foundation for decision-making based upon what would have done under similar circumstances. In other words, the fiduciary, as the person delegated to carry on a responsibility of the parent, is to apply the perspective and values of the individual who delegated the decision-making authority, not necessarily the fiduciary's own perspective and values.

Estate Planning Attorneys

In addition to selecting guardians, personal representatives, executors and pre-need guardians it is also important to choose the right estate planning attorney.

Selecting the right estate planning attorney for you means doing your homework—educating yourself, defining your needs, learning to value professional services and seeking guidance in the selection of a qualified individual. Proper estate planning, especially for unmarried couples and same-sex partners, revolves around your relationship with your estate planning attorney.

Unfortunately, there are many businesses and salespeople masquerading as estate planning professionals. They are inundating the public with sales schemes that involve selling wills, living trusts and other estate planning directives without the involvement of attorneys in the counselling, design and drafting of the plan and, ultimately, the preparation of the directives. Their approach is based on a transaction mentality—once you've signed your newly created estate plan, you are done. There is no discussion of the need for ongoing counselling, updating, support and maintenance. Likewise, there is no information being provided regarding the costs of updating, maintaining and then, ultimately, the administration of the estate of the person for whom the plan was created.

Proper estate planning requires professional thoroughness by attorneys and other advisors, and respect for the overall well-being of the client and the client's family. Your attorney should aspire to the highest ethical professional behavior that will lend dignity to you, your family and the planning process.

As you evaluate your needs and begin the search for a qualified attorney, consider the following:

What is an attorney? Attorneys are known by many different names, such as lawyer, counselor or counsellor, solicitor and advocate. Attorneys are required to obtain extensive educational training in order to be prepared and able to represent a client. To qualify to practice law, attorneys must earn a law degree—referred to as a Juris Doctor or J.D.—pass a state bar examination and commit to pursuing continuing legal education for the duration of their legal career.

Attorneys are subject to codes of ethical conduct and professional responsibility imposed by their state bar associations. Generally, the profession as a whole self-monitors its members. Attorneys can be sole practitioners, members of small firms or members of large firms. An attorney can be an associate, of counsel or a partner. Attorneys can be general practitioners or attorneys can specialize in a particular area of the law. You should seek an attorney who concentrates his or her practice in estate planning with particular experience in planning for life alliance partners.

Attorneys can be plaintiff oriented or defense oriented. They can be trial attorneys, called litigators, with a practice that focuses on trial work, or they can be transactional lawyers who concentrate on some of the non-litigation aspects of the law, such as corporate, real estate or estate planning. Then, there are attorneys who refer to themselves as "relationship oriented" attorneys because they are not merely interested in a client for a single transactional event, but desire an ongoing mutually rewarding and beneficial relationship with their clients.

Selecting an attorney will depend on many different factors—not the least of which is the purpose for which you are interviewing attorneys in the first place. It is important to think about attorneys in the same context as doctors. You wouldn't hire your family practitioner or a gynecologist to conduct brain surgery despite the fact they have the same underlying educational foundation! Additional training and years of specialization are determining factors in selecting the right professional for your legal needs.

Selecting the right attorney is critical. However, just seeking a competent attorney is often not enough. Consider the personal qualities your attorney should have before you start interviewing candidates. Things you should look for:

- Scrupulous honesty and integrity
- Sensitive and perceptive communication
- Good judgment and common sense
- Discipline and toughness

- Creativity in finding constructive solutions
- Bar affiliations, designations, advanced training, specialization

What does "board certified" mean? Board certification is a voluntary designation program for attorneys. Certification requirements vary depending on your state and the area in which the attorney is seeking certification. Certification often requires additional continuing legal education requirements and may require the applicant to pass a certification examination. There may be additional requirements: that the attorney practice in the area of specialty for a number of years; devote a required percentage of his or her practice to the specialty area; handle a variety of matters in the area to demonstrate experience and involvement; attend ongoing continuing education; obtain favorable evaluations by fellow lawyers and judges; and pass a written examination.

Board certification will give you some indication of the attorney's competence in the area for which you are seeking legal advice. This is not to imply that attorneys who are not board certified do not have high levels of competence. Many highly qualified attorneys have chosen for personal or professional reasons not to seek board certification. It does not in any way diminish their qualification or commitment to excellence in their selected practice area.

Why do I even need an attorney? Can't I do an estate plan on my own? You can try. Many have. Everyone already has an estate plan, whether they know it or not. As we have mentioned several times in preceding chapters, if you fail to plan, the laws in your state of residence will identify the individuals qualified to make decisions for you in the event of your disability or the disposition of your assets in the event of your death. For unmarried life alliance partners, this is a very risky proposition, as most state laws don't contemplate the rights of unmarried partners.

For some individuals, joint ownership of assets is the only step they've taken toward creating an estate plan. An estate planning attorney can help you avoid some of the pitfalls of the estate planning decisions you might have made or might make.

However, if you ask, "Does a 'do-it-myself' plan work for my partner and/or my family?" and you answer, "No," then you have made progress in recognizing that the laws of the United States are complex and you should seriously consider the guidance and advice of a professional. It pays to select your estate planning professional with care, since you will not survive to see whether your plan succeeds, and your loved ones will live with the results.

Your legal professional has spent thousands of dollars and years of time learning how to analyze problems and distinguish the simple from the complex. Finding a simple solution to a complex problem has as much value as unraveling a complex situation that may appear simple. Professionals add value to their services by their knowledge, skill and wisdom, continuing education, independent perspective and willingness to take responsibility for the results.

Okay, you've convinced me, I need an attorney. How do I find the one that will be best for me? This is a serious but not necessarily difficult task. First, consider recommendations from friends and other attorneys. Personal referrals are generally the best way to find out about any type of service you might need, and legal representation is no exception. Talk to other people who are similarly situated. If you belong to any local organizations, consult with other members to obtain a referral. Ask your banker, your CPA, your financial advisor or your current legal services provider. Attorneys rely on good client relations and word of mouth reference for referral business. If you don't have any success getting a personal referral, consider local or state bar associations or other legal referral services.

The Martindale Hubbell Law Directory is one recognized source of information about attorneys. There are many other directories that list attorneys. However, remember that the attorneys listed in many directories have paid a fee for the privilege of being listed there.

As a last resort, let your fingers do the walking and search your local yellow pages. However, understand that you should not make your selection of attorney based solely on yellow page advertising in the attorney section—if such advertising is permitted in your state. You need to thoroughly consider to whom you should entrust your estate planning.

What kind of questions should I ask? You should ask questions pertinent to your particular area of concern, and you should focus on the following:

- What is your experience in this field?
- Have you handled matters like mine?
- What are the possible problems or concerns in situations like mine?
- How long do you expect this matter to take?
- How will you communicate with me?

- Will you be my only contact, or will anyone else be working with you?
- Is there a charge for the initial consultation?
- Do you offer educational workshops on the subject?
- How do you handle your legal fees? Do you charge by the project? Do you charge a percentage? Do you charge by the hour? What is your hourly rate?
- Beyond fees, what types of expenses should I expect to incur?
- If I need to make changes, how will the fees be handled?
- When will I pay? How often will I receive a bill? If fees are not paid on time, will interest accrue?
- What alternative recommendations can you make regarding my choices or my course of action?
- Will I sign a formal fee or engagement agreement?
- In the event of a dispute, do you recommend mediation, arbitration or litigation?

Attorney Fees and Costs

With regard to legal fees and costs, it is important to understand the fees and billing arrangement before you get a bill. Attorneys' fees can vary dramatically depending on the nature and scope of the legal services provided. The scope of the representation is an understanding as to what the attorney will do (or not do), how long it will take, what the attorney will not do without further authorization, what the client's goals are, and so forth. Financial arrangements should be as clear as possible, unless doing so would take longer than whatever it is the attorney is being retained to do. Even then, the maxim is to "put it in writing."

Some attorneys provide services on a flat-fee or quoted-fee basis while others provide services based on an hourly calculation, which becomes a function of the attorney's (and his or her staff's) hourly billing rate multiplied by the number of hours expended on your behalf. If you have legal needs of an ongoing nature, will the attorney agree to a retainer fee agreement where you pay a fixed fee each month for services? Are costs included in the quoted fee or will they be in addition to any quoted amounts? Are there any other add-ons, like legal research fees, paralegal costs, long distance phone charges or facsimile and copy charges?

There are a number of factors that may enter into the calculation of attorneys' fees. Some attorneys, like personal injury attorneys or workers' compensation attorneys, charge on a contingency basis or a percentage of the recovery obtained on your behalf. Others may charge on an hourly basis or on a project basis.

Higher hourly fees generally coincide with a lawyer's experience and/or geographic location. For example, an attorney in Los Angeles, Chicago, New York City or Washington, D.C., is likely to charge a higher hourly rate than a comparable attorney in a smaller city. Likewise, the size of the firm may dictate higher hourly rates for both partners and associates than a smaller firm in the same location. Other factors that play into higher fees are the cost of rent, salaries for support staff and firm "perks," or benefits.

Generally, fees are negotiable, although, as a rule, not after the services have been provided. If you intend to negotiate with your attorney for the value of the services provided, it would be best to initiate that conversation prior to the onset of the representation. Some attorneys may be offended by the notion they would consider negotiating their fees.

As with any other situation where you will be contracting for professional services, it is recommended you obtain, review and execute a fee agreement or engagement letter that clearly outlines the scope of the representation provided and the billing arrangement you've agreed to. Make sure you understand your rights with regard to termination of the relationship and what will happen in the event of a dispute between you and your attorney. Further, make sure you understand how long the attorney intends to maintain your file. Does the attorney have any processes or procedures for keeping you updated in the event the law changes with regard to the services that have previously been provided? Our experience is that most relationships with an attorney are based on a transactional basis. This means the legal relationship for representation purposes is terminated when the scope of the transaction is completed.

How do I make sure my attorney and I have a good relationship? Good legal assistance and advice is not a one-way street. You have to cooperate with your lawyer if you genuinely want him or her to help you. The attorney-client relationship is privileged and confidential, so you need to take a lawyer into your confidence. Here are some important tips:

1) Don't withhold information from your attorney. In the field of estate planning, it is critical your attorney know everything about you and your loved ones including all of your hopes, dreams, fears, aspirations, eccentricities and peccadilloes. Your attorney needs to know what it is

like to be you or a member of your family. What does life look like for your loved ones if you are disabled or if you pass away? What assets do you own, how do you own them and who are the named beneficiaries? What type of planning have you done in the past? Without all of this information, the attorney will be unable to assess your situation, educate you about the law and how it affects you, your partner and your family, and achieve a result that will be in your best interest.

2) Don't expect simple or immediate answers to complicated questions. Attorneys are justifiably cautious in drawing conclusions or answering complex legal questions without consideration of all the relevant facts. An attorney knows there can be a number of answers to the same question and the law is rarely an open, and, shut case. Attorneys have also been trained to closely examine both sides of an argument. You may find that attorneys frequently use lawyer words like, "it depends," "possibly," "could be" and "there is a great likelihood." Rarely will attorneys use statements such as "guaranteed," "always" and "never." There are frequently a large number of factors that can cause any situation to have an unintended or unexpected outcome.

3) Keep your attorney advised of all new developments. In order to do a good job, your attorney needs to be apprised of facts that may have changed in your personal or financial situation. When your attorney has all the facts, he or she can use this information to provide you with relevant information regarding changes in the law or the attorney's experience.

4) Never hesitate to ask your lawyer about anything you believe is relevant to your situation. Your attorney cannot read your mind. Also, remember that attorneys are not psychiatrists, doctors, marriage counselors or financial advisors. You will still need a team of trusted advisors to provide you with answers to all of your relevant questions and concerns.

5) Follow your attorney's advice. You asked for it. You paid good money for it. Don't work against your attorney.

6) Be patient. Don't expect instant results. Trust your attorney to follow through and follow up, but don't hesitate to ask for periodic progress reports. You have a right to know exactly what your attorney is doing for you. If you've engaged the services of an estate planning attorney who practices utilizing a formal estate planning process, you should always know what to expect next.

7) Your attorney's primary duty is loyalty to you. His or her interest is protecting your rights and providing you with the highest possible quality of service. Early consultation with an attorney can save you trouble, time and money because:

- The solution to your legal situation may be easily resolved or prevented depending on the nature of your problem.
- The earlier you seek competent advice, the less time is generally needed to complete the work required.

Information is generally more readily available when prompt action is taken. Within the estate planning realm, this may be especially important in the event a person becomes mentally disabled, becomes catastrophically ill or dies before they have completed their planning.

Many legal matters or strategies are time sensitive or may have a statute of limitations. Failure to act in a timely manner may prevent you from acting at all.

What other things should I consider? Experience. The length of time an attorney has been in practice is an important indicator of his or her success and ability to adequately handle your legal matter. Most attorneys require between three and five years of experience before they have gained reasonable competence in a particular area of the law. Does the attorney regularly attend continuing education on the subject matter? Does he or she teach locally, regionally or nationally? Is he or she published? A good indicator of a person's mastery of a subject is their ability to teach it or to write about it.

Background. Does the attorney have any specific background or experiences that provide him or her with a unique perspective on your situation? Many attorneys are "second career" individuals who may have worked in other professional areas prior to attending law school. This past professional experience may be used to add significant expertise to their area of practice.

Comfort. How does the attorney make you feel? Do you feel comfortable and understood? Does the attorney speak in terms and use language you can understand? Does he or she take the time to explain those questions that are still unclear to you?

Work Load. What is the attorney's work load? A common misconception is that an attorney with a cluttered desk is unorganized and has too much work to do an adequate job. Ask the attorney how many clients he or she is currently handling. Does the attorney feel overwhelmed by the work load or outside commitments? What other projects is he or she working on? What are his or her outside interests? Do you feel rushed? Is the attorney taking the time to fully answer all questions regarding your situation? Has the attorney explained the retainer or fee agreement? Do you feel pressured to sign the retainer and run out of the office?

Past Results. Past results are never a guarantee of future success, but knowing an attorney's track record or experience in your type of situation can provide added comfort if he or she has had continuing success in cases similar in nature to yours.

Malpractice Insurance. Some states and some state bar ethics rules require that attorneys include information in their retainer agreements as to whether they carry malpractice insurance. Malpractice insurance is designed to protect you from negligence or intentional behavior of your attorney.

If information concerning the malpractice insurance carried by your attorney is not included in your written retainer agreement, ask that it be included. If an attorney does not carry malpractice insurance, you may pay lower fees, however, if a material mistake is made on your case which affects the case's outcome, you may have legal recourse but no ability to recover financial damages from the attorney's personal resources.

Imagination. Does your attorney have the ability to imagine ways in which something might go wrong? In the estate planning area, we incorporate a philosophy of "planning for the worst and hoping for the best" because any other kind of plan is simply wishful thinking. If something can go wrong it will, and Murphy's Law generally ensures that the one thing that was not planned for is the one thing that will happen.

Skill. Skill includes familiarity with the law, with a technical field or with legal procedures. Skill cannot be taken for granted. Although different attorneys have different skills and skill levels, *any* attorney is legally permitted to handle any legal matter, so long as: 1) there is no conflict of interest; 2) the attorney can handle the matter competently (generally a matter of opinion—the attorney's); and 3) All other laws and rules of professional conduct are followed.

Like other skilled professionals, attorneys develop skills in specific areas of practice. An attorney who is very skilled at matters of type X may need to climb a steep learning curve to properly handle a matter of type Y. Beware of general practitioners or those who have a threshold practice because these individuals, although they may be very good at some legal matters, may not have the specific expertise you need or require. We have discovered that many attorneys, regardless of their practice area, feel competent to draft a simple will. Our experience has been and continues to be that there is no such thing as a simple estate plan, especially when there are unmarried couple and same-sex partner issues, only clients and professionals who don't fully understand the enormity of the problem.

Intuition or "Good Instincts." Intuition may arise from previous encounters with a judge, an opposing attorney or some other decision-maker in the matter at hand. Intuition can give an attorney a sense of how a decision maker is likely to react to various arguments being considered by the attorney. There may be no way to determine whether someone has good intuition, except to rely on your own intuition.

Good Character. This concept is complementary to intuition but of course, reputation can be helpful as well.

Other factors that will also be important include the resources available to the attorney, the time frame in which the attorney can attend to your matter, and so on. However, ultimately you must be comfortable with your attorney, because your attorney cannot help you unless you communicate with each other. Choose someone you respect, not someone who intimidates you or uses jargon when it isn't needed. Your calls should be answered promptly and professionally. You should not feel as if conversations with your attorney are being either rushed or dragged out. If you are not comfortable, let your attorney know. If the relationship doesn't improve, look elsewhere.

What if I can't afford a lawyer? Don't assume you can't afford a lawyer. Investigate the matter with competent legal counsel first. In many instances, the cost of competent legal advice now can save you hundreds, if not thousands, of dollars later. If you still feel you can't afford legal help, you may want to consult your local legal aid society.

Summary

Don't discount the value in seeking out organizations and professionals who dedicate themselves to the specialty practice area for which you need advice. In the arena of planning for life alliance partners, this means someone who can devote the time to understand the unique needs of the partners.

Selecting your personal representative, trustees, attorneys and/or other team members is going to be a critical part of the success of your estate plan. Be sure that you give attention to each detail of your plan and then implement your plan to accomplish your goals.♥

Chapter 10

The Paper Trail —
Asset Integration and Funding

Life alliance partners must keep records of any number of things:

- Documents for assets or debts brought to the relationship and acquired during the relationship
- Receipts and other records memorializing any items of value they gave to each other
- Copies of income tax returns and gift tax returns
- Originals of life alliance agreements
- Originals of any legal directives
- Location lists setting forth their assets, the locations of important papers and the names of advisors or others who need to be contacted if something should happen to either partner
- Insurance policies and copies of the beneficiary forms
- Any receipt, return, contract or item they would need to satisfy the IRS or state taxing authorities regarding the assets and transactions the partners engaged in while partners
- Memorial instructions and copies of prepaid funeral contracts

Asset Integration

Asset integration refers to the process of making sure your assets have the appropriate legal title and legal directives in order to control the management of the assets during disability and distribution at death. This area of planning requires good communication between the partners and their legal and financial advisors. A misstep in one area of planning can inadvertently undo a decision in another area of planning.

An error or omission regarding the title or disposition of a particular asset can cause the best legal directives to fail to achieve the partners' goals. For instance, if the partners buy life insurance as a means to create immediate funds to support the survivor, naming the owner's estate as the beneficiary will not achieve this goal. The partners should get clear instructions from their team of advisors and make sure the advisors are working in a coordinated way.

Funding Trusts

If a trust is used as the planning solution, the documents confirming that the trust owns the assets should be kept with the original trust. The special steps required to make sure the trust instructions control assets are set forth below.

Any trust that has no assets earmarked to fund it is essentially worthless. Steps must be undertaken to make certain the trust is funded with assets designed to meet the needs of the trustmaker during lifetime and the intended beneficiaries in the event of disability or death. Funding a trust means that legal title to the trustmaker's assets are changed into the name of the trust. It may also mean renaming beneficiary designations on contract assets like insurance policies, annuities and retirement plans.

The creation of the legal documents for an estate plan is only the first step in the process. There must be sufficient assets, properly owned, in order to make sure the instructions contained in the trust will be carried out for the ultimate benefit of the beneficiaries.

It is at this stage of the planning process that the team concept of professional advisors becomes most critical. The lawyer can create the legal framework, but it is now up to you, in concert with your professional team, including a CPA and financial advisor to construct a financial plan consistent with the goals and resources that will best suit the unique needs of your family.

Like lawyers, there are few financial advisors who have experience planning for the future of life alliance partners. The average financial planner is trained to look at the overall estate and try to provide as many dollars as possible, while at the same time keeping an eye out for potential problems. If uninformed, the financial advisor may use a traditional approach to addressing the needs of the partners and may trigger unintended consequences for them.

Transferring assets into the trust requires either a change of legal ownership of the asset during your lifetime or naming the trust as beneficiary at the death of the owner of life insurance and/or retirement plans or other beneficiary designated assets. The advisors should be familiar with the potential tax consequences of such transfers and alert the partners to them. The partners may make informed decisions to accept those consequences or they may chose to forgo a particular solution for tax or other reasons.

The financial advisor should help the partners make sure they have not overlooked sources of assets, such as military benefits with survivor options. Insurance has been described as a perfect mechanism for families to either create wealth or to cover the cost of taxes on wealth. Insurance can be a method to leverage smaller premium amounts in order to leave a large lump sum for the future benefit of the surviving life alliance partner.

The specific amount required to adequately fund the trust for the future needs of the life alliance partner and other family members is personal to each family and requires a detailed financial plan with projections about returns on investments.

A trust can hold almost any kind of asset or can be the recipient of any kind of asset that is payable on death of the asset owner. Although some trusts hold title to no assets until the death of the trustmaker, it is generally recommended that at least a minimum amount be placed in the trust to fund it initially.

Assets can be added to the trust over time. Additions may be made by gifts during life, by will or trust, by life insurance policies, by employee plan benefits, or by retirement plan benefits.

Where to Keep Important Papers

Originals of important papers should be kept in a fireproof and waterproof box or safe. Additional consideration should be given to the type of box or safe if there is concern for theft or tampering with the contents. A safety box kept at home that can be carried off won't be helpful.

Safe deposit boxes in banks are sometimes a good place to keep important papers. You will need to make individual decisions about whether to keep items in a safe deposit box and who will have authority to access the box. In some instances, it may be advisable for a revocable living trust and the corresponding trustees to be the lessees on a safe deposit box to ensure that any subsequent trustees will also have access to the box. Whether a bank safe deposit box meets the needs of the partners depends on a number of factors. One concern with regard to safe deposit boxes is that they may not be accessible when it is important to have immediate access to their contents. This may be especially true if you keep healthcare directives in your safe deposit box and there is a medical emergency on the weekend or on a holiday.

The long-standing rule in many states was that state law required the bank to freeze access to the box when an owner died to permit the state tax-auditing authority time to audit the box contents. The rationale for this policy was to prevent family members from removing jewelry, negotiable instruments or other liquid assets before the tax auditors could include their value in the probate estate. Many states have relaxed the tight restraints on immediate access and permit bank officials to perform a preliminary audit of box contents after which the contents are released to an authorized person.

Sometimes there may also be concerns of some family members that someone gaining early access might not share the contents with others or that a will or other legal directive might be destroyed if it was not favorable to the person gaining access. The rules for intestate succession will apply if there was no will and assets were in the deceased partner's individual name or there are other types of assets but no other legal directives, such as beneficiary designations or trusts.

Some attorneys will keep the original will or other legal directives in their firm's safe or bank deposit box. Generally, this is a mechanism to enhance the likelihood that the survivors will retain the lawyer to probate the will. However, you need to determine what happens to the documents if the attorney becomes ill or passes away or if you lose contact with the attorney's office. Your loved ones will need to know whom to contact if you haven't provided them with information about who is the custodian of the documents.

Many firms, however, do not retain originals, but only copies, of the documents they have prepared for the client. Therefore, the need to find a safe place for the other documents in the paper trail still must be satisfied. As a general rule, our firms do not retain original documents, unless specifically requested to do so. In addition, we advise that clients keep their documents at home in a safe but accessible place.

Probate courts in most jurisdictions have a repository for wills. For a small, one-time fee, a will is deposited with the court and kept confidential until the will-maker dies. At that point, the will can be admitted to probate.

If changes to the will are made, the amended or replacement wills can also be filed in the repository and cross-referencing of the filing numbers is possible. This is a way for a person to feel secure that the will can be located and submitted to the probate court at their death.

If the will-maker moves to another state, decisions must be made about updating the will in the new jurisdiction and informing the first repository that the will on file is no longer current. Part of the paper trail includes clear notes when original plans have been changed. These factors should be discussed with legal advisors to arrive at the best solutions for your situation.

Partners should retain copies of their important papers with explicit instructions as to where the originals can be located. In this age of electronic records, copies on a compact disc (CD) are particularly handy for the computer literate. Obviously, some understanding of the proper storage and handling of such mechanisms is important, as well.

A location list can be essential for survivors trying to recall specific locations of originals and copies of various assets. In some respects, a location list is a thoughtful gift from the deceased partner. It conveys the thought and attention the partner had for the peace of mind and well-being of the survivor. For many of our clients, we provide a comprehensive, tabbed and organized notebook that includes pre-printed information regarding the identification of legal documents and assets that allows the trustmaker to further customize the list as to the exact location of many items. This notebook serves as a resource center for survivors and others as to the location of many important planning directives.

Summary

Life alliance partners should consider creating a system for tracking their gifts and expenditures, acquisition prices and contributions by each partner regarding assets. This tracking system will streamline preparation of tax returns, will be useful for establishing "basis" for purposes of determining capital gains taxes and can help you respond to potential challenges from taxing authorities regarding the contributions from each. An ongoing system will help you avoid the necessity of trying to reconstruct documents and transactions from memory. This might also help you avoid some unnecessary disputes if your relationship should terminate for other reasons prior to death.

The daily financial interactions between unmarried partners produce many potential tax consequences. The tax laws treat the financial interactions between a married couple much more favorably. Therefore, the paper trail for unmarried couples is essential. ♥

Chapter 11

Keeping it All Together—
Updating, Education and Maintenance

*E*state planning is viewed by some as a single transaction, something you do and then don't have to worry about any more. In addition, the initial planning process may have been emotionally traumatic for the family and it isn't an experience they want to have to repeat. You may be surprised to learn, then, that all estate planning requires ongoing updating, maintenance and family education. Creating the plan is simply the first step in a lifetime process.

There are a number of factors that can influence an estate plan over time:

- Changes in your family or financial circumstances.
- Changes in the law, both state and federal, that may affect the long-term operation of your plan.
- Changes in your attorney's experience.

Changes in Your Family or Financial Circumstances

The first type of change an estate plan faces is change that directly affects you and your family, both personal and financial. There is no way for your attorney and other planning professionals to learn about these changes unless you tell them.

These can pose a major threat to the plan if advisors are not aware of them.

The National Network of Estate Planning Attorneys informally polled its clients and discovered that, on average, people update their estate plans every 19.6 years! Has anything changed in the last 20 years that may have affected your estate plan? the last 10 years? the last 5 years? How about in the last year? Estate plans that don't work as expected result in loss of benefits for loved ones, can result in litigation and, at worst, may cause family turmoil that undermines the structure of the family.

Our experience has been that most people don't communicate regularly with their professional advisors, thereby putting their estate plan in danger of failing. Sometimes, people are discouraged from communicating with their professional advisors because of the actual or perceived cost of communicating changed circumstances. In other words, people tend to communicate with their advisors less when they know there is an invoice attached.

Changes in the Law

The second type of change an estate plan faces is change to either state or federal laws, including the tax laws with its limitations and restrictions or other laws that can affect the personal planning protections provided in your estate plan. The tumultuous changes in the laws governing the rights of life alliance partners requires regular updating to stay current with the opportunities and potential threats to their rights.

Changes in Your Advisor's Experience

The third type of change an estate plan faces is change in your attorney's or professional advisor's experience. Many professionals are committed to constantly improving their practices, their knowledge and the quality of their planning. Others continue to practice the same way they always have. Does your attorney have years of cumulative experience or is he or she still doing things the same old way? In Chapter 9—Fiduciaries, Attorneys and Other Scary People, look for guidance on evaluating your attorney's commitment to excellence.

An Estate Planning Solution—The Three Step Strategy™

It's not about documents—it's about results! The key to proper estate planning is clear, comprehensive, customized instructions for your own care and that of your loved ones. These instructions can be included in a will, in a trust and in several other related legal directives. Regardless of the type of planning chosen, most people are best served with an estate planning process that revolves around the Three Step Strategy™. The Three Step Strategy is an approach to planning that recognizes that certain processes have to be firmly in place to create estate plans that work!

The Three Steps

Step 1) Work with a Counselling-Oriented Attorney (as opposed to a word processing-oriented attorney). Much of what passes for estate planning in this country today is little more than word processing! We don't believe you should pay a licensed professional to fill out forms or to do only word processing. The value of a professional is in his or her counsel and advice, based on knowledge, wisdom and experience. If word processing is all you want, you might as well do it yourself! But if you want a plan that works, seek good counselling. (Note: we've incorporated the old English spelling for "counselling," which denotes an approach that focuses on the role of attorney as advisor and counsellor at law.)

Step 2) Establish and Maintain a Formal Updating, Maintenance and Education Program. An estate plan faces a myriad of changes. First, there is constant change in your personal, family and financial situation. Second, there are inevitable changes in both federal and state laws that impact your estate plan. Third, there is (or should be) ongoing change in your attorney's experience and expertise. Your professional advisors should be continually improving their performance and expanding their knowledge through ongoing education and collective experience. Since everything, except human nature, constantly changes, you cannot expect a plan to accomplish what it is intended to accomplish if it is never updated. The costs of failing to update your plan are typically far greater than the costs of keeping your plan current.

If your attorney doesn't offer a formal updating, maintenance and education program, discipline yourself to review your plan on a systematic basis. As you prepare to have your annual tax return prepared, this is a good time to get out your estate planning documents and review them with your professional team. Financial advisors generally offer or require annual reviews with their clients. This gives you a good opportunity to review the performance of your financial portfolio and to discuss and measure whether your investment strategy is still consistent with your long-term goals.

Your family assets should be reviewed on a regular basis to make certain that distributions made during life or upon death will not trigger unintended taxes that your loved ones cannot pay. Meet with your attorney on a regular basis, not to exceed two years, to review your personal estate plan. Include your life alliance partner and other key family members in these meetings, especially those individuals selected to serve as personal representatives, executors or trustees so they can begin the education process and understand the legal issues they may face in the future. Families who take the time to develop a long-term relationship with their legal advisors, who learn and understand the legal concepts that affect their family and who have a commitment to make sure their plan stays updated and maintained have fewer problems when a family crisis arises and estate plans need to be implemented.

Step 3) Assure Fully Disclosed and Controlled Settlement Costs after Your Death. The cost of any estate plan has three distinct parts:

- Today's Cost: This is what you pay today for counselling and design (or for word processing);
- The Cost Over Time: This is what you pay over time for updating, or the potentially larger cost of failing to update;

- The After-Death Cost: This is the cost paid by your loved ones for settlement, administration and distribution of your assets. Regardless of the plan you choose (a will, a trust, beneficiary designations), there are always after-death costs. Wills are administered through probate; trusts have to be settled or administered. In either case, assets must be transferred to their intended beneficiaries and final income tax or estate tax returns must be prepared. Be sure you discuss and understand all three parts of the cost of your estate plan with your attorney before you begin to plan.

Unfortunately, most people only focus on today's costs and often select planning options based on that figure. As a result, they can overlook the updating costs (or the costs of failing to update) and the after- death estate administration costs. Understanding all of the costs associated with your options and asking how they can be controlled will help you select the option best suited for your personal financial circumstances.

The Importance of the Team Approach

Estate planning decisions straddle legal, financial and other advisor categories. Sometimes advisors give conflicting advice—not because the advice is necessarily wrong, but because there can be several ways to achieve a planning goal and the advisors all look at the goal from their own planning perspective, a form of planner "tunnel vision." Tunnel vision, however, can cause unintended consequences.

An example might occur when a non-legal advisor recommends that a parent add an adult child's name to the parent's bank account as a strategy to avoid probate. The parent, child and non-legal advisor might not fully understand that the joint account is potentially subject to the child's creditors if the child faces divorce or lawsuit. Under the circumstances, the parent might select a different method to avoid probate.

Sometimes it can seem there are too many options to consider. Some advisors call this "analysis paralysis" to describe the confusion and inaction their clients can experience when there seems to be too many choices. Creating an estate plan is not difficult, but it does require a commitment on your part as well as the involvement of all your professional advisors: your attorney, your accountant and your financial and insurance advisors. Depending on your plan, it may also require the participation of a planned giving professional for the charitable organization(s) of your choice.

You should discuss with the advisors how you would like them to work together to help you find the best solutions for your situation. Some advisors are very familiar and comfortable with working in a collaborative way to assist their clients. Other advisors may not have had many collaborative experiences. If an advisor is not open to this method, it might say something about whether you will be comfortable with him or her as an advisor.

You should keep your advisors informed of the steps you are taking so each can bring his or her expertise to the process. This will help you eliminate planning tunnel vision and unintended outcomes. If all of the professionals are included in the planning, you are far more likely to have an estate plan that works; in other words, a plan that meets your goals and keeps you in control of the process and the results.

Ethical Considerations

All of your advisors, but particularly attorneys, must address their ethical duties to each partner. The rules that govern attorneys require them to zealously represent the interests of their client. If an attorney represents more than one client on the same matter, conflicts of the partner's interests can present themselves. You need to know how the attorney will handle those situations without compromising his or her duty to zealously represent you and your partner's interests.

The conversation regarding an advisor's ethical obligations should address:

- Whose interests the advisor represents
- How the advisor will present options when the options might give an advantage to one partner at the expense of the other
- Who pays the advisor
- What happens if a conflict of the partners' interests occurs
- The scope and manner of disclosure of information to other advisors and to the partners

The partners should receive a written confirmation of the details of the ethical obligations and normally will be required to sign a consent form if the advisor represents them both. It is advisable for partners to retain separate advisors when there is a significant disparity between the partners' wealth, health or extended family, since these factors generally will create potential conflicts of interest.

Creating an estate plan that works requires commitment. It also requires an acknowledgment that the plan you create today may not be the plan you need (or want) in the future. Life is dynamic. Your estate plan should be, too. This has never been more true than in the current climate of planning for unmarried partners.

Some of the specific planning solutions and theories currently being used for life alliance partners have been discussed throughout the book. Keep in mind, however, that these options do not exist in a vacuum. New legal solutions can be created by weaving existing legal principles, like the ones discussed in Chapter 2, with new statutes and court decisions coming in from various jurisdictions. ♥

Chapter 12

The End of the Road or Part of the Journey?

The legal and societal turmoil that currently surrounds the issues of unmarried couples and same-sex partners is not likely to be resolved soon. However, we don't see this as the end of the road, just the continuance of the journey.

Until life alliance partners can legally claim for themselves some of the protections offered to married couples, you will have to be diligent in creating and incorporating those legal techniques, directives and devices that will provide you and your partner with the greatest possible protections. We hope we have provided some guidance, direction and insight into how you might best accomplish your objectives.

At a minimum, we suggest you protect yourselves with a comprehensive, well-conceived and competently designed estate plan. The plan should include as its foundation, a will or a trust, durable financial powers of attorney, powers of attorney for healthcare matters, living wills, pre-need guardian declarations and memorial instructions. You will also be well served to understand that asset ownership controls the disposition of assets, and then carefully coordinate your asset ownership with your estate plan. In addition, we highly recommend you consider crafting a life alliance agreement that will outline the asset ownership issues for you and your partner both during your lifetime and in the event your relationship should end. If you own business or creative projects, make sure those assets are protected, as well.

In addition to ownership issues, don't overlook the indebtedness that you and your partner may co-obligate yourselves to. It is just as important to understand how liabilities will be shared as it is to outline the ownership of the assets the debt supports. Don't make assumptions about entering into joint debt obligations without fully understanding your rights and obligations.

Prepare disability directives including your health care power of attorney, living will and pre-need guardian declaration so that your loved ones are properly appointed to make important health care related decisions. In addition, be sure to share your feelings so they are also fully informed regarding your decisions regarding heroic care.

Determine whether probate and estate tax avoidance are worthy goals as part of your estate plan. Understand the complexities associated with probate, as well as its costs, and create your estate plan in a way to minimize this proceeding without sacrificing protections for your partner and your family. Often, being penny-wise today results in pound-foolishness for the future.

Consider advanced planning or business techniques such as ILITs, family foundations, limited liability companies and buy-sell agreements as tools that can assist you in accomplishing gifting and tax-minimization goals. Be sure these legal mechanisms are consistent with your willingness to include a level of complexity into your estate plan. Many advanced planning techniques can accomplish family goals, but are destined to fail if there is no commitment or formal process undertaken on the part of the family, the advisors and the successors to keep the mechanism current.

We don't want you to use this book as a do-it-yourself guide for creating these legal directives on your own. Instead, use it as an educational tool so you can arm yourself with knowledge in order to make informed decisions. We have always subscribed to the tenet of "educate to motivate," and that's what we hope we have accomplished here.

Choose your trusted advisor team carefully. Select an estate planning attorney conversant in life alliance partner planning. Choose a financial advisor and certified public accountant who understand the special investment and tax concerns of life alliance partners. Ensure that all parties are well-schooled in the special concerns of life alliance partners. Then, be sure your advisors are willing to work in a collaborative environment that has you at the center—with all parties working toward one common goal: the achievement of your objectives with your best interests at heart.

Educate your partner, your family and your named successors regarding their expected roles in your plan. Surprises at disability or death are never appreciated. Share the information you feel comfortable sharing and then ensure that your successors will carry out your directives. Utilize corporate fiduciaries or other professionals if you aren't confident your family can rise to the administrative and emotional challenge of carrying out your wishes.

Estate planning, like the issues surrounding life alliance partners, is a life-long journey. There is nothing static about an estate plan. Your plan needs to be updated and maintained consistently over time to take into consideration the very dynamic legal environment we all live in. Without constant care and attention, your best efforts today may result in frustration and legal entanglements in the future. Our goal is to help you protect yourselves.

We wish you good health, a long life and relationships filled with love. ♥

Appendix A

Glossary of Estate Planning Terms

Administrator — Person named by the court to administer a probate estate. Also called an Executor or Personal Representative.

Agent — An individual named in a power of attorney with authority to act on the power giver's behalf. Has a fiduciary responsibility to the power giver.

Ancillary Administration — An additional probate in another state. Typically required when you own assets or real estate in a state other than the state where you live that is not titled in the name of your trust or in the name of a joint owner with rights of survivorship.

Basis — What you paid for an asset. Value used to determine gain or loss for capital gains and income tax purposes.

Buy-Sell Agreement — A written agreement between co-owners of a business to determine the rights of the owners in the event of retirement, disability or death.

Co-Trustees — Two or more individuals who have been named to act together in managing a trust's assets. A Corporate Trustee can also be a Co-Trustee.

Corporate Trustee — An institution, such as a bank or trust company, that specializes in managing or administering trusts.

Disclaim — To refuse to accept a gift or inheritance so it may be transferred to the next recipient in line. Must be done within nine months of the date-of-death.

Durable Power of Attorney for Financial Matters — A legal document that gives another person full or limited legal authority to make financial decisions on your behalf in your absence. Valid through mental incapacity. Ends at revocation, adjudication of incapacity or death.

Durable Power of Attorney for Healthcare — A legal document that gives another person legal authority to make health care decisions for you if you are unable to make them for yourself. Also called Healthcare Proxy, Healthcare Surrogate or Medical Power of Attorney.

Estate Administration — The process of settling either a probate estate or trust estate. There are generally three steps that include identifying the assets, paying the debts of the estate and distributing the balance to the beneficiaries.

Executor — Another name for Personal Representative.

Fiduciary — Person having the legal duty to act for another person's benefit. Requires great confidence, trust, and a high degree of good faith. Usually associated with a Trustee or Personal Representative.

Funding — The process of re-titling and transferring your assets to your Living Trust. Also includes the re-designation of beneficiaries to include your Living Trust as a beneficiary. Sometimes called asset integration.

Inter vivos — Latin term that means "between the living." An *inter vivos* trust is created while you are living instead of after you die. A Revocable Living Trust is an *inter vivos* trust.

Irrevocable Life Insurance Trust (ILIT) — An irrevocable trust for the purpose of holding title to life insurance. Used as an advance planning technique to remove the death benefit proceeds of life insurance from an insured's gross taxable estate.

Irrevocable Trust — A trust that cannot be changed or canceled once it is set up. Opposite of Revocable Living Trust. Can be created during lifetime or after death.

Intestate — Dying without a Will.

Joint Ownership — When two or more persons own the same asset.

Joint Tenants with Right of Survivorship — A form of joint ownership where the deceased owner's share automatically and immediately transfers to the surviving joint tenant(s) or owner(s).

Living Trust — A legal entity created during your life, to which you transfer ownership of your assets. Contains your instructions to control and manage your assets while you are alive and well, plan for you and your loved ones in the event of your mental disability and give what you have, to whom you want, when you want, the way you want at your death. Avoids guardianship of the property and probate only if fully funded at incapacity and/or death. Also called a Revocable *Inter Vivos* Trust.

Life Alliance Agreement — A written agreement between two life alliance partners for the purpose of establishing ownership to property, rights and obligations with regard to property and disposition of property in the event of the termination of the relationship.

Life Alliance Partner — A life partner of the same or opposite-sex in a committed relationship.

Limited Liability Company (LLC) — A form of legal entity that can provide limited liability from the claims of creditors. Can be taxed as a sole proprietorship, partnership, s-corporation or c-corporation.

Living Will — A legal document that sets forth your wishes regarding the termination of life-prolonging procedures if you are mentally incapacitated and your illness or injury is expected to result in your death.

Personal Representative — Another name for an Executor or Administrator.

Pour Over Will — An abbreviated Will used with a Living Trust. It sets forth your instructions regarding guardianship of minor children and the transfer (pour over) of all assets owned in your individual name (probate assets) to your Living Trust.

Power of Attorney — A legal document that gives another person legal authority to act on your behalf for a stated purpose. Ends at revocation, incapacity (unless it is a durable power of attorney) or death.

Probate — The legal process of validating a Will, paying debts, and distributing assets after death. Generally requires the serves of an attorney.

Probate Estate — The assets owned in your individual name at death (or beneficiary designations payable to your estate). Does not include assets owned as joint tenants with rights of survivorship, payable-on-death accounts, insurance payable to a named beneficiary or trust, and other assets with beneficiary designations.

Probate Fees — Legal, executor, court, and appraisal fees for an estate that requires probate. Probate fees are paid from assets in the estate before the assets are fully distributed to the heirs.

Revocable Living Trust — Another name for a Living Trust.

Spendthrift Clause — Protects assets in a Trust from a beneficiary's creditors.

Successor Trustee — Person or institution named in a trust document that will take over should the first Trustee die, resign or otherwise become unable to act.

Testamentary Trust — A Trust created in a Will. Can only go into effect at death. Does not avoid probate.

Testate — An estate where the decedent died with a valid Will.

Trust Administration — The legal process required to administer trust assets after incapacity or death. Includes the management of trust assets for the named beneficiaries, the payment of debts, taxes or other expenses and the distribution of assets to beneficiaries according to the Trust instructions. Generally requires the services of an attorney.

Trustee — Person or institution who manages and distributes another's assets according to the instructions in the Trust document.

Will (or Last Will & Testament) — A written document with instructions for disposing of assets after death. A Will can only be enforced through the probate court.

Appendix B

Estate Planning Checklist

Part 1—Communicating Your Wishes

☐ **Yes** ☐ **No**   Do you have a will?

☐ **Yes** ☐ **No**   Are you comfortable with the executor(s) or trustee(s) you have selected?

☐ **Yes** ☐ **No**   Have you executed a living will or healthcare proxy in the event of catastrophic illness or disability? Is your life alliance partner prominently named in these documents as your surrogate for decision making purposes?

☐ **Yes** ☐ **No**   Have you executed a durable financial power of attorney for the purpose of appointing an agent to handle your financial affairs in the event of your disability?

☐ **Yes** ☐ **No**   Have you considered a revocable living trust to consolidate assets, avoid probate, minimize exposure to estate tax and provide long-term protections for your life alliance partner and other family members?

☐ **Yes** ☐ **No**   If you have a living trust, have you titled your assets in the name of the trust? Have you named your trust as the primary beneficiary on your contract assets? ie. insurance, annuities, and retirement plans.

☐ **Yes** ☐ **No**   If you have a will, trust or other legal directives, have they been reviewed in the last two years to ensure they are consistent with your wishes, the status of the law and your attorney's changing experience?

Part 2—Protecting Your Family

☐ **Yes** ☐ **No**   Does your will name a guardian for your minor children?

☐ **Yes** ☐ **No**   Does your estate plan specifically include provisions to protect your life alliance partner in the event of your death?

☐ **Yes** ☐ **No**   Are you sure you have the right amount and type of life insurance to help with survivor income, loan repayment, capital needs and estate-settlement expenses?

☐ **Yes** ☐ **No**   Have you considered an irrevocable life insurance trust to exclude the insurance proceeds from being taxed as part of your estate?

☐ **Yes** ☐ **No**   Have you considered creating trusts for either your life alliance partner or the family to facilitate gift giving?

Part 3—Helping to Reduce Your Estate and Income Taxes

☐ **Yes** ☐ **No**   Do you and your life alliance partner each individually own enough assets for each of you to qualify for the applicable exclusion amounts, currently $1.5 million?

☐ **Yes** ☐ **No**   Are both your estate plan and your partner's designed to take advantage of each of your applicable exclusion amounts, currently $1.5 million?

☐ **Yes** ☐ **No**   Are you making gifts to your partner or other family members that take advantage of the annual gift tax exclusion, currently $11,000?

☐ **Yes** ☐ **No**   Have you gifted assets with a strong probability of future appreciation in order to maximize future estate tax savings?

☐ **Yes** ☐ **No**   Have you considered charitable trusts that can provide you with both estate and income tax benefits?

Part 4—Protecting Your Business

☐ **Yes** ☐ **No**   If you own a business, do you have a management succession plan?

☐ **Yes** ☐ **No**   Do you have a buy-sell agreement for your family business interests?

☐ **Yes** ☐ **No**   Is your life alliance partner employed by your business? Have you taken all steps necessary to ensure his or her continued participation in the business in the event of your death?

☐ **Yes** ☐ **No**   Have you considered a gift program that involves your family-owned business?

Endnotes

1. U.S. General Accounting Office correspondence regarding the effects of the Defense of Marriage Act (DOMA).
2. Human Rights Campaign (Washington, D.C. advocacy group for gay, lesbian, bisexual and transgender people).
3. *Goodridge v. 172. of Public Health*, 440 Mass. 309 (2004-022).
4. Black's Law Dictionary, 4th Edition.
5. Ibid.
6. Ibid.
7. Ibid.
8. Ibid.
9. See *Trammel v. United States*, 445 U.S. 40, 44 (1980).
10. *Hewitt v. Hewitt*, 394 N.E. 2d 1204 (1979).

About the Authors

PEGGY R. HOYT, J.D., M.B.A. Peggy is the oldest of four daughters born to John and Trudy Hoyt. She was born in Dearborn, Michigan, and spent her first ten years as a "PK," or "preacher's kid," before her father joined The Humane Society of the United States. Peggy graduated with an A.A. degree from Marymount University in Arlington, Virginia; earned a B.B.A. and M.B.A. from Stetson University in DeLand, Florida; and earned a J.D. from Stetson University College of Law in St. Petersburg, Florida.

Today, Peggy and her law partner, Randy Bryan, own and operate Hoyt & Bryan, LLC. Her law firm limits its practice to estate planning and administration for individuals, married couples and life alliance partners, including special needs planning, pet planning, elder law and guardianships. She also works in the areas of business creation and succession, as well as real estate, corporate transactions and equine law.

Peggy is the author of a one-of-a kind book called *All My Children Wear Fur Coats—How to Leave a Legacy for Your Pet,* available through her law office, your favorite bookstore or by visiting www.legacyforyourpet.com. In addition, she and Candace Pollock are co-authors of a recently released book, *Special People Special, Special Planning—Creating a Safe Legal Haven for Families with Special Needs* also available through their law offices, your favorite bookstore or by visiting www.specialpeoplespecialplanning.com.

She is active in a variety of organizations, including the National Network of Estate Planning Attorneys, as a regular speaker on estate planning topics and contributor of practice management materials. In addition, she serves as trustee to Stetson University's Business School Foundation and as a board member of The Harmony Institute and Friends of Winter Miles, not-for-profit animal-related organizations.

Peggy's passion is her pets and she enjoys spending her "free" time playing with her wild mustang horses, Reno and Tahoe, and her Premarin rescue, Sierra; her dogs, Kira, Corkie, Tiger and Fiona; and her cats, Beijing, Bangle, Cuddles, Tommy, Shamu and Spook.

By the time this book goes to print, Peggy will have married her long-time life alliance partner, Joe Allen. Peggy and Joe live in a rural community outside Orlando, Florida

---

CANDACE M. POLLOCK, J.D. Prior to attending law school, Candace owned a business that provided claim review and consulting services to Ohio lawyers in the area of workers' compensation and Social Security claims - areas involving the rights of disabled people. During this period she was a founding member and first acting president of the Women Business Owner's Association (now known as the Cleveland Chapter of the National Association of Women Business Owners).

Candace graduated from Cleveland-Marshall College of Law and is a principal in HAHN & POLLOCK, LLC.

Candace continued to represent the interests of disabled people while expanding her practice to include estate and financial planning, probate and elder law services in response to the needs of her clients. Her practice focuses on the unique planning needs of unmarried partners, the disabled and the elderly.

Her participation in professional and community activities includes leadership roles in legal and professional associations: Chair of the Workers' Compensation and Social Security Section of the Cuyahoga County Bar Association, Representative-at-Large on the Board of Trustees of the Ohio Academy of Trial Lawyers (OATL) and Member-Executive Committee of the Workers' Compensation Section of OATL. She participates in non-board positions in other non-profit, charitable and political organizations and is currently a mentor coach in the Practice Builder Program of the National Network of Estate Planning Attorneys (NNEPA).

In addition to her professional and community activities, she teaches individuals and organizations and writes about various estate and disability planning topics. This is her second book.

Candace resides in Cleveland, OH with her life alliance partner, Hutch and their family of animals.♥

Contact Us

Peggy and Candace are available as speakers and for interviews and are happy to contribute written material to publications regarding planning for life alliance partners. Please feel free to contact them at:

HOYT & BRYAN, LLC
251 Plaza Drive, Suite B
Oviedo, Florida 32765
(407) 977-8080 (T)
(407) 977-8078 (F)
peggy@HoytBryan.com
www.HoytBryan.com

HAHN & POLLOCK, LLC
820 West Superior Avenue,
Suite 510
Cleveland, Ohio 44113
(216) 861-6160 (T)
(216) 861-5272 (F)
info@HAHNPOLLOCK.com
www.HAHNPOLLOCK.com

Or visit their web site designed especially for you and your life alliance partner at www.lovingwithoutalicense.com.

Please also visit www.domesticpartnerlawyeralliance.com for more information on attorneys across the United States who provide estate planning services for life alliance partners.

Other Planning Concerns

Pets. For information related to planning for your pets, please visit www.legacyforyourpet.com

Special Needs. If you have a special needs family member, please visit www.specialpeoplespecialplanning.com.♥

Printed in the United States
21799LVS00004B/136